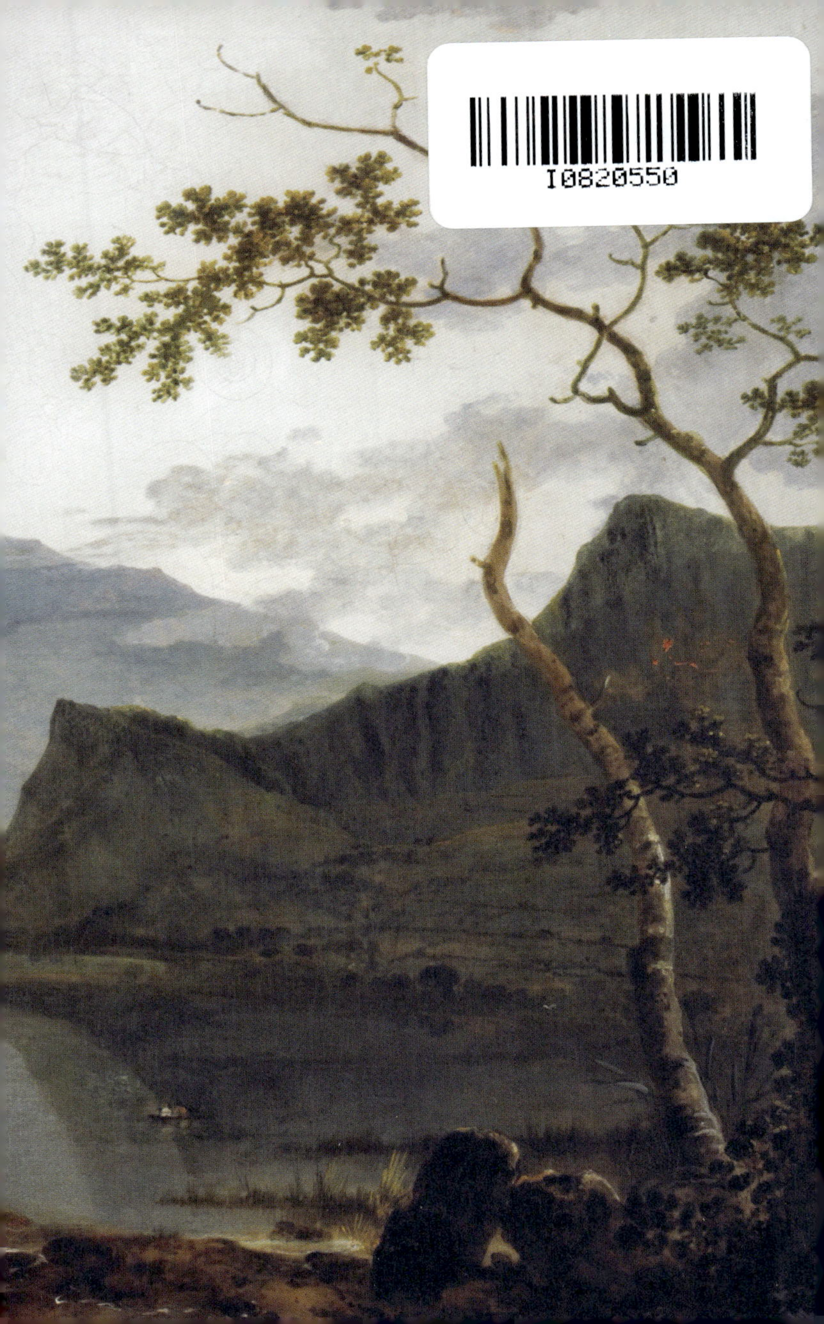
I0820550

Dame **Margaret Drabble** is an English novelist, biographer and critic. She is the author of nineteen novels, including *A Summer Bird-Cage* (1963), *The Millstone* (1965), *The Peppered Moth* (2001) and *The Dark Flood Rises* (2016), and was the editor of *The Oxford Companion to English Literature* (1985, 2000). Among many accolades, in 1973 she became a Fellow of the Royal Society of Literature, and in 2011 she received a Golden PEN Award for a Lifetime's Distinguished Service to Literature.

POCKET PERSPECTIVES

Surprising, questioning, challenging, enriching: the Pocket Perspectives series presents timeless works by writers and thinkers who have shaped the conversation across the arts, visual culture and history. Celebrating the undiminished vitality of their ideas today, these covetable and collectable books embody the best of Thames & Hudson.

MARGARET DRABBLE ON THE ROMANTICS

With 11 illustrations

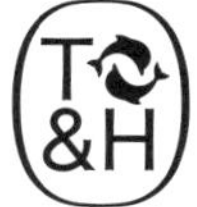

This book consists of extracts from *A Writer's Britain* by Margaret Drabble, originally published by Thames & Hudson in 1979 and released in an updated edition in 2009.

Front cover and endpapers: Richard Wilson, *Snowdon* [Yr Wyddfa] *from Llyn Nantlle*, 1765–66. Oil on canvas, 101 × 127 cm (39¾ × 50 in.). Walker Art Gallery, Liverpool (WAG 2429).

First published in the United Kingdom in 1979 in *A Writer's Britain* by Thames & Hudson Ltd, 181A High Holborn, London WC1V 7QX

First published in the United States of America in 1979 in *A Writer's Britain* by Alfred A. Knopf, Inc.

This abridged edition published in the United Kingdom in 2025 by Thames & Hudson Ltd, 181A High Holborn, London WC1V 7QX

This abridged edition published in the United States of America in 2025 Thames & Hudson Inc., 500 Fifth Avenue, New York, New York 10110

Margaret Drabble on The Romantics
© 2025 Thames & Hudson Ltd, London
Text © 1979 and 2025 Margaret Drabble

All Rights Reserved. No part of this publication may be reproduced or transmitted in any form or by any means, electronic or mechanical, including photocopy, recording or any other information storage and retrieval system, without prior permission in writing from the publisher.

British Library Cataloguing-in-Publication Data
A catalogue record for this book is available from the British Library

Library of Congress Control Number 2024951334

ISBN 978-0-500-02949-7

Impression 01

Printed in China by Shenzhen Reliance Printing Co. Ltd

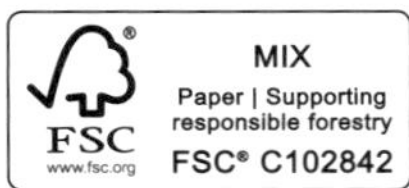

CONTENTS

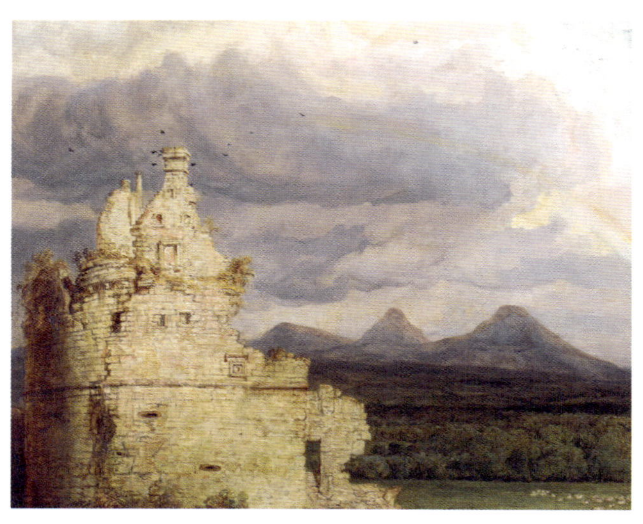

1. James Ward, *The Eildon Hills and The Tweed* (detail), 1807. Oil on panel.

PREFACE

LANDSCAPE IN LITERATURE

I FIRST EMBARKED on *A Writer's Britain* in 1979, prompted by the photographer Jorge Lewinski. I felt myself to be exploring, what was to me, a very new subject. It was a journey of discovery, encouraging me to read widely and speculate about the strengths of British landscape writing, in poetry and in prose. It was a very happy journey. Since then, writing about nature and landscape has flourished conspicuously in the work of Robert Macfarlane, Sara Maitland, Iain Sinclair, Roger Deakin, Sarah Moss, Michael Symmons Roberts and many others. New words have been added to our literary vocabulary, such as 'psychogeography' and 'edgelands'.

Landscape occupies a peculiar and special place in British literature, which is rich in evocations of what Shakespeare proclaimed as 'this other Eden, Demi-Paradise'. Indeed, at the beginning of the nineteenth century, love of nature seemed almost to replace love of God or mankind as a subject for literature. Despite an uncertain climate and a large-scale industrial revolution, British writers – and painters – have persisted in seeing and praising the distinctive beauties of the country. Generations of exiles have longed for the green fields of home, and expressed their longing in their own words, or the words of others. Even the cynical Lord Byron could not suppress a surge of enthusiasm at the sight of the white cliffs of Dover and the green fields of Kent. Many travellers returning from grander, wilder, more picturesque scenery may feel the same delight.

The Romantic movement was the most complete expression of this sense of the importance of place, and William Wordsworth was its genius. It is difficult to appreciate, more than two hundred years later, how vastly our sensibilities were changed at the dawn of the movement. The word 'landscape' itself is relatively new, dating from the end of the sixteenth century; the word 'scenery' is even more recent, dating from the late eighteenth century. Both are now so familiar that it is hard to imagine how writers managed without them. The interweaving of the visual arts, literature and place are part of our heritage.

The American novelist Nathaniel Hawthorne, visiting the Lake District in 1855, astutely comments in his *English Notebooks* that 'every point of beauty is so well known, and has been described so much, that one must needs look through other people's eyes, and feel as if he were seeing a picture rather than a reality'. I argue that seeing places through the eyes of writers is part of what gives us recognition and delight. Those who enjoy reading gain great pleasure from associating places with lines of poetry, with scenes from novels. One pleasure reinforces the other. Even those who do not read much cannot choose but see certain landscapes through the eyes of the writers that discovered them. The vision of countless visitors who have never read a word of Walter Scott has been formed by Scott's poems and novels. Knowingly or unknowingly, we have all been influenced by the writers who went before us, and the popularity of the great literary shrines of Britain shows how irresistibly many are drawn to retrace, in the most literal sense, their footsteps.

Another of the attractions of landscape lies in the fact that it represents at once the changing and the unchanging. Places on the whole change more slowly than people, and nothing evokes the past more powerfully than a visit to the remembered places of childhood. Many writers see in a pond, a field, a tree, a church some reminder of what they once were. Sometimes the journey to the past ends in disappointment: how can one ever find the farm near Knutsford that Elizabeth Gaskell describes with such intensity of feeling? To most of us today, Knutsford is a service station on a motorway, and Cranford is a town of the mind. Yet there are places that remain unchanged; the moors behind Haworth remain for now much the same as when Emily Brontë walked them. Tintern Abbey has suffered successive waves of restoration and dilapidation, but the valley of the Wye itself is still recognizable as the valley that Wordsworth first saw as a young man. Since *A Writer's Britain* was first published, stretches of the River Wye have become notorious for phosphate pollution, and a by-word for habitat destruction, but the Abbey and its memories and its literary associations survive. The legacy of the Romantics still animates and inspires us.

Margaret Drabble
2024

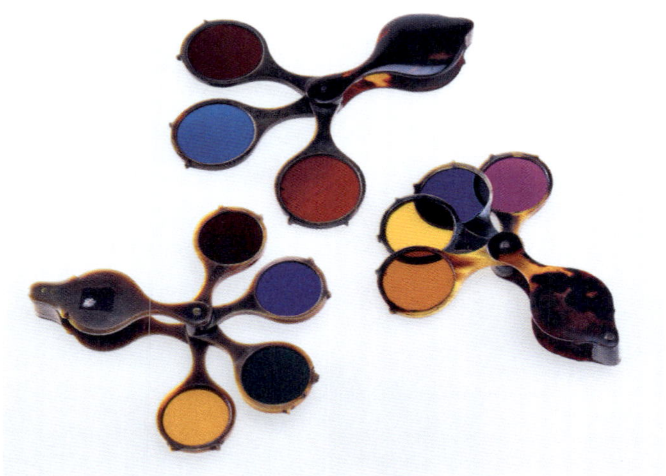

2. Claude Lorrain glasses, 1800–24. Coloured viewing glasses used by landscape painters.

THE ROMANTICS

The eighteenth century on the whole preferred to view nature through a Claude glass or a drawing room window: to compose it, to organize it, and to avoid (except in verse) its more violent manifestations. In one decade, Wordsworth swept away the antiquarian aestheticism of the past, replacing it with a feeling of passionate urgency and deep involvement. The snowbound shepherds of Thomson's 'Winter' belong to a different order from those in Wordsworth's *Prelude*. Wordsworth's moments of revelation by the dark lake are different in kind from Gray's reflections in a country churchyard: his daffodils dancing by the lake at Grasmere have nothing to do with Thomas Warton's April vision of 'the vegetable blaze of Flora's brightest 'broidery'. Wordsworth forged a new relationship between man and the natural world: he lived in a new communion, and when he was young he found the language, in Shelley's phrase, like clay in his hands.

He was, as he himself many times declared, fortunate in his birth. His was an exceptionally lovely part of the country: his subject matter lay around him in his infancy. The river Derwent and the mountains of Cumberland were as mother and father to him. Despite travels and wanderings, some happy, some tormented, he knew that the Lake District was his home; like Constable, with whom as an artist he has much in common, he felt that his own landscapes had formed him, and he returned there to work as soon as he could find the means. Unlike Thomson, who moved to London when opportunity called, or Goldsmith, who wrote of deserted villages while frequenting taverns in Fleet Street, Wordsworth needed to live what he believed; he was no weekend enthusiast, but a man who saw the integrity of the life and of the work. His own life style, of 'plain living and high thinking' has become an image in itself.

As we have seen, the Lakes had already been 'discovered' as picturesque some time before Wordsworth's birth in 1770, and no doubt had he never been born tourists would still flock to visit them, but it is through his eyes that we see them, not through the calculating eyes of Gilpin or the apprehensive ones of Gray. Wordsworth was not a tourist, but a native of the region, and knew intimately the places he describes; they were the images of his childhood, the associations of daily life. His poetry had made each place he mentions a place of pilgrimage, and he has probably added more names than any other writer to a literary map of England: Grasmere, Esthwaite, Cockermouth, Derwentwater, Rydal Mere, Patterdale, Hawkshead, Ullswater, Windermere, Helvellyn – the list is endless. Yet he is in no sense a descriptive writer, content to catalogue outward appearances. Nor does he use natural description as an excuse for moralizing on the state of the nation. For him, the landscape is the message, and he himself is the landscape. It is not fanciful to see in him and his work the qualities of the region that reared him, for he himself was constantly seeking such affinities, seeking the animate in the inanimate, with a persistence that goes far beyond traditional anthropomorphism. Born into a grand setting, he had grand ambitions: frequently he compared his own ambition to a star, a mountain peak.

Wordsworth's attitude to nature was not a fixed creed; it changed and developed. As a small boy, he tells us, he enjoyed 'the animal pleasures' – bathing naked in the Derwent, climbing crags for birds' nests, boating, fishing, skating. But this idyllic freedom was clouded over from time to time by darker portents, and he was troubled by 'grave and serious thoughts'; in the famous episode of the stolen boat, in Book 1 of *The Prelude*, he tells us that the sight of the huge cliff which reared up from the lake and seemed to stride after him like a living thing disturbed him deeply:

> ... and after I had seen
> That spectacle, for many days, my brain
> Work'd with a dim and undetermin'd sense
> Of unknown modes of being; in my thoughts
> There was a darkness, call it solitude,
> Or blank desertion, no familiar shapes
> Of hourly objects, images of trees,
> Of sea or sky, no colours of green fields;
> But huge and mighty Forms that do not live
> Like living men mov'd slowly through my mind
> By day and were the trouble of my dreams.

As he grew older, he was drawn to the grander and darker aspects of nature – to Burke's 'Sublime' – and was later to reproach himself for the enthusiasm with which he had pursued them, almost as though reproaching himself for seeking too violent a stimulant, too powerful a drug. One of his many tributes to his sister Dorothy gives her the credit for curing him of this excess. In Book 13 of *The Prelude* he writes:

> In nature and in life, still to the last
> ...
> I too exclusively esteem'd that love,
> And sought that beauty, which, as Milton sings,
> Hath terror in it. Thou didst soften down
> This over-sternness; but for thee, sweet Friend,
> My soul, too reckless of mild grace, had been
> Far longer what by Nature it was framed,
> Longer retain'd its countenance severe,
> A rock with torrents roaring, with the clouds
> Familiar, and a favourite of the Stars:
> But thou didst plant its crevices with flowers,
> Hang it with shrubs that twinkle in the breeze,
> And teach the little birds to build their nests
> And warble in its chambers.

It is perhaps significant that this softening process took place largely in the milder region of the West Country Quantocks, in the first youth of the Wordsworths' friendship with Coleridge: significant, also, that he clings to his faith that nature herself had appointed him as the

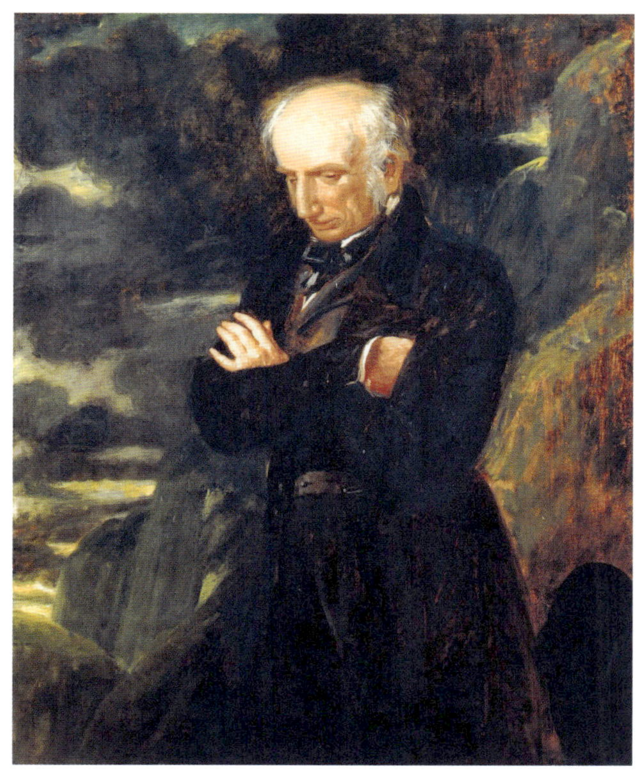

3. Benjamin Robert Haydon,
William Wordsworth (or *Wordsworth on Helvellyn*), 1842. Oil on canvas.

familiar of rocks and mountains. Dorothy, not nature, taught him to see the violet by the mossy stone, but she conceded his feeling for the Sublime, and named 'the lonesome peak' of Stone Arthur, near Grasmere, after him:

> ... 'Tis in truth
> The loneliest place we have among the clouds.
> And She who dwells with me, whom I have loved
> With such communion, that no place on earth
>
> Can ever be a solitude to me,
> Hath to this lonely Summit given my Name.

It is also interesting that Wordsworth managed to find the bleak aspects even in Somerset and Devon; while Coleridge was writing of jasmine and bean flowers, and Dorothy of glittering miles of grass, of green ferns in waterfalls, of springing wheat and turnips, Wordsworth wrote of hail storms and the stunted thorn that became the centre of one of his most austere ballads, *The Thorn*.

It is impossible, in this space, to do justice to the complexity and originality of Wordsworth's contribution to the literature of landscape. He painted place as it had never been painted before, and connected it in new ways with man's thought processes and moral being. Many of his descriptions are indeed severe and terrible: take this passage in *The Prelude*, where he describes the experience of losing his father. It is Christmas time, the holidays are about to begin, and Wordsworth impatiently climbs a crag to look for the horses that will carry him and his brother home:

> … 'Twas a day
> Stormy, and rough, and wild, and on the grass
> I sate, half-shelter'd by a naked wall;
> Upon my right hand was a single sheep,
> A whistling hawthorn on my left, and there,
> With those companions at my side, I watch'd,
> Straining my eyes intensely, as the mist
> Gave intermitting prospect of the wood
> And plain beneath. Ere I to School return'd
> That dreary time, ere I had been ten days
> A dweller in my Father's House, he died
>
> …
>
> And afterwards, the wind and sleety rain
> And all the business of the elements,
> The single sheep, and the one blasted tree,
> And the bleak music of that old stone wall,
> The noise of wood and water, and the mist
> Which on the line of each of those two Roads
> Advanced in such indisputable shapes,
> All these were spectacles and sounds to which
> I often would repair and thence would drink,
> As at a fountain; and I do not doubt
> That in this later time, when storm and rain
> Beat on my roof at midnight, or by day
> When I am in the woods, unknown to me
> The workings of my spirit thence are brought.

This is a remarkable analysis of the interaction of place and emotion, of past and present, of reality and imagination. Never since Shakespeare has scenery been made to bear such a weight of significance.

Wordsworth lost both his parents while still a child: his mother died when he was seven, his father when he was eleven. His dual attitude to nature – seeing her both as stern mentor and consoling nurse – seems to be related to these two vanished figures: the grand, dark landscapes are associated with the admonishing father, the homely images of the sunny river and the beloved vale of Esthwaite and the green valley of the Wye with his mother and his sister.

Wordsworth not only saw the natural world as a vital formative influence on man; he was at least half persuaded that every living object, even plants and trees, could experience joy and sorrow. The world was a living symbol, but more than that, it lived in its own right. At times he seems to recognize that this pantheistic approach is half fantasy, half pathetic fallacy: he speaks of the poet who, 'pleased within his own passions and volitions is delighted to contemplate similar volitions and passions as manifested in the goings-on of the Universe, and *habitually impelled to create them where he does not find them*' (my italics). He was much mocked by more rational contemporaries in parodies like *The Simpliciad* for his 'breathing blossoms' and his 'twigs that pant with pleasure'. Yet what he says is tentative enough: it is his *faith*, he says, 'that every flower enjoys the air it breathes', and of the budding twigs he writes:

And I must think, do all I can,
That there was pleasure there ...

– the qualifying phrase 'do all I can' implying that he is trying to be rational, but, in the pull of so much spring happiness, failing. His outpouring is spontaneous, deeply felt, utterly different in quality from such poems as Cowper's 'The Yardley Oak', in which the poet appoints himself 'oracle' for the tree and speaks through its imagined history.

Wordsworth and Coleridge felt in their bones a natural piety: it was a crime against the living universe to kill wildlife. (Wordsworth regretted his boyhood birds-nesting, though he continued to fish.) Both wrote poems about the consequences of idle slaughter: the albatross in 'The Rime of the Ancient Mariner' and the hart in 'Hart-Leap Well' are memorable symbols, the more memorable in an age of hunting and shooting. Dorothy taught Wordsworth that it was a crime to kill a butterfly or uproot a strawberry plant. We hear more now of the possible feelings of small creatures and plants, but in their day such an approach was unusual: Gilbert White of Selborne, fondly though he observed the worm and the snake, felt no inhibition against killing them through scientific curiosity. It is true that many of Wordsworth's poetic predecessors had taken pleasure in personifying the vegetable kingdom: James Hurdis in *The Village Curate* celebrates the 'martial pea', 'the gay bean' and the 'soporific lettuce', and Erasmus Darwin in his *Loves of the Plants* was firmly committed to the idea that plants could feel, and for that reason preferred insectivorous, climbing and sensitive plants, such as *Mimosa*, which seemed 'almost human' to him. He particularly loved sundew, *Drosera*, as did his grandson Charles, who was to write to his friend Charles Lyall, 'I care more about *Drosera* than the origin of all the species in the world.' 'That wicked dear little Drosera' was very dear to the younger Darwin. Yet Erasmus Darwin's playful ascribing of sexual passions to flowers and vegetables is largely a literary device, a charming and novel way of conveying botanical information. Wordsworth half meant what he said.

I am beginning to think that one of the reasons why Wordsworth called forth so deep a response is that he was drawing on deep sources of collective feeling, on a primitive animistic view of the world, certainly present in earlier times, but powerfully suppressed by the scientific seventeenth and eighteenth centuries. The child and peasant see inanimate objects and natural forces as possessed of a life of their own. Wordsworth was able, like Freud in later days, to restore an essential contact with the primitive, to divine its workings, and to restore an earlier vision. Man, cut off from nature by centuries of rationalism, was restored to her bosom. Yet Wordsworth makes no grand claims. When he writes of his sister,

> ... Her the birds
> And every flower she met with, could they but
> Have known her, would have lov'd ...

he is not claiming that birds and flowers can possess human knowledge; they would, if they could. Flowers and birds no longer speak, as they did in fairy tales and legends: something of paradise is lost. Yet we can still make contact with the mighty Being that animates the universe: Wordsworth, sitting under the sycamore in the valley of the Wye above Tintern, looking at the 'wild green landscape' and the little farms and hedgerows, can declare in 'Tintern Abbey':

> ... And I have felt
> A presence that disturbs me with the joy
> Of elevated thoughts; a sense sublime
> Of something far more deeply interfused,
> Whose dwelling is the light of setting suns,
> And the round ocean and the living air,
> And the blue sky, and in the mind of man;
> A motion and a spirit, that impels
> All thinking things, all objects of all thought,
> And rolls through all things.

Similarly, on his ascent of Snowdon, he seems almost to see and hear 'The Soul, the Imagination of the whole':

> ... I looked about, and lo!
> The Moon stood naked in the Heavens, at height
> Immense above my head, and on the shore
> I found myself of a huge sea of mist,
> Which, meek and silent, rested at my feet:
> A hundred hills their dusky backs upheaved
> All over this still Ocean, and beyond,
> Far, far beyond, the vapours shot themselves,

In headlands, tongues and promontory shapes,
Into the Sea, the real Sea, that seem'd
To dwindle, and give up its majesty,
Usurp'd upon as far as sight could reach.

This is the kind of landscape that had not appeared in English since Milton, and, after it, it was difficult to look upon nature as a prettily arranged prospect, subject to man's domination.

It has been since Roman times a commonplace to claim that the shepherd's life is better than the courtier's, the country purer than the town. Wordsworth seriously believed this. He saw the city as a contaminating force, an imprisonment; many times he pities Coleridge for his deprived childhood, 'in city pent'. Wordsworth was one of the few who knew shepherds in real life, and had observed their domestic and working lives. Critics have complained that he reads his own feelings into them, and thus elevates them unnaturally, but Wordsworth makes it clear that he knows he is tempted to do precisely this: he tends to see them in superhuman terms, he says, because this is how they presented themselves to him as a child:

Seeking the raven's nest, and suddenly
Surpriz'd with vapours, or on rainy days
When I have angled up the lonely brooks
Mine eyes have glanced upon him, few steps off,
In size a giant, stalking through the fog,
His Sheep like Greenland Bears; at other times
When round some shady promontory turning,

His Form hath flash'd upon me, glorified
By the deep radiance of the setting sun:
Or him have I descried in distant sky,
A solitary object and sublime,
Above all height!... Thus was Man
Ennobled outwardly before mine eyes ...

A far cry this, in setting and sentiment, from the oaten stops, pastoral songs and garlanded nymphs of Arcadia. Similarly, in 'Michael, A Pastoral Poem', he admits that he first loved shepherds

... not verily
For their own sakes, but for the fields and hills
Where was their occupation and abode.

Not much pretence here; nor in a cancelled draft of the same poem, where he says of the old shepherd:

No doubt if you in terms direct had ask'd
Whether he lov'd the mountains, true it is
That with blunt repetition of your words
He might have stared at you, and said that they
Were frightful to behold, but had you then
Discours'd with him in some particular sort
Of his own business, and the goings on
Of earth and sky, then truly had you seen
That in his thoughts there were obscurities,
Wonders and admirations, things that wrought
Not less than a religion in his heart.

This is great poetry, and profound knowledge. Wordsworth was so rich in both that he could afford to discard such lines.

I see that my own bias has combined with Wordsworth's and that, inevitably, I have stressed the Sublime rather than the homely in his nature and his work. Wonderfully though he conveyed the huge panorama and the grand view from the mountain top of effort, he was equally good at the precise observation, at the 'little unpretending rill', the withered celandine, the bird's nest. Indeed, there was something in him that seemed increasingly to fear the loneliness and exposure of the lofty summits of his own fame, that sought as he grew older the steady lake, the moss-grown garden, the kettle whispering its faint undersong by the half-kitchen half-parlour fire. It was Dorothy who encouraged these milder, safer pleasures, and his debt to his sister is fully revealed in her *Journals*, which have a rare, and in her day new, delicacy of natural observation. How many thousands of nineteenth-century country ladies followed in her footsteps, making notes, sketching, recording their own lonely and incommunicable feelings, and the year's changes. Dorothy was bad at drawing, unlike many well-educated girls of her time, but her descriptions are sensitive to every change of mood and weather, reflecting a delicate inner balance between the two.

Like her brother, she had strong views on the naturalness of nature, and the folly of interfering with it. In 1798 she records a visit to a garden in the neighbourhood of Alfoxden, where they were then living, in these terms:

> April 15th. Walked about the squire's grounds. Quaint waterfalls about, about which Nature was very successfully striving to make beautiful what art had deformed – ruins, hermitages, etc, etc. In spite of all these things, the dell romantic and beautiful, though everywhere planted with unnaturalised trees. Happily we cannot shape the huge hills, or carve out the valleys according to our fancy.

She was equally censorious a few years later on a visit to Windermere, on 8 June 1802:

> Ellen and I rode to Windermere. We had a fine sunny day, neither hot nor cold. I mounted the horse at the quarry. We had no difficulties or delays but at the gates. From the High Ray the view is very delightful, rich and festive, water and wood, houses, groves, hedgerows, green fields and mountains; white houses, large and small. We passed 2 or 3 nice-looking statesmen's houses. Mr Curwen's shrubberies looked pitiful enough under the native trees. We put up our horses, ate our dinner by the water-side, and walked up to the Station. Then we walked to the Island, walked round it, and crossed the lake with our horses in the Ferry. The shrubs have been cut away in some parts of the Island. I observed to the boatman that I did not think it improved. He replied, 'We think it is, for one could hardly see the house before.' It seems to me, however, no better than it was. They made no natural glades; it is merely a lawn with a few

> miserable young trees, standing as if they were half-starved. There are no sheep, no cattle upon these lawns. It is neither one thing or another – neither natural nor wholly cultivated and artificial, which it was before. And that great house! Mercy upon us, if it could be concealed, it would be well for all who are not pained to see the pleasantest of earthly spots deformed by man.

She felt much more at home in her own valley, by her own lake of Grasmere, and her *Journal* is full of descriptions of her walks – for, like her brother, she was a great walker, and was reprimanded in childhood for her unladylike fondness for rambling alone. The lake seems at times a mirror to her soul: on parting with her dear brother, 'The lake looked to me, I knew not why, dull and melancholy, and the weltering on the shores seemed a heavy sound ...' (14 May 1800). In happier mood (with William) she reports, 'The lights were very grand upon the woody Rydale hills. Those behind dark and topped with clouds. The two lakes were divinely beautiful. Grasmere excessively solemn and the whole lake was calm, and dappled with soft grey ripples' (20 October 1800). With William again, on 15 April 1802 she saw the immortal daffodils:

> When we were in the woods beyond Gowbarrow Park we saw a few daffodils close to the water-side. We fancied that the lake had floated the seeds ashore, and that the little colony had so sprung up. But as we went along, there were more and yet more; and at last,

> under the boughs of the trees, we saw that there was a long belt of them along the shore, about the breadth of a country turnpike road. I never saw daffodils so beautiful. They grew among the mossy stones about and about them; some rested their heads upon the stones as on a pillow for weariness; and the rest tossed and reeled and danced, and seemed as if they verily laughed with the wind ...

Her height of happiness is achieved in the company of William and Coleridge on a walk on a hot day in May:

> We almost melted before we were at the top of the hill. We saw Coleridge on the side of the water; he crossed the Beck to us ... William and I ate a luncheon, then went on towards the waterfall. It is a glorious wild solitude under that lofty purple crag. It stood upright by itself. Its own self, and its shadow below, one mass – all else was sunshine. We went on further. A Bird at the top of the crags was flying round and round, and looked in thinness and transparency, shape and motion like a moth. We climbed the hill, but looked in vain for a shade, except at the foot of the great waterfall, and there we did not like to stay on account of the loose stones above our heads. We came down, and rested upon a moss-covered rock, rising out of the bed of the river. There we lay, ate our dinner, and stayed there until about 4 o'clock or later. William and C. repeated and read verses. I drank a little Brandy and water and was in Heaven.

black and green, the birche
here & there greenish but
there is yet more of pur
to be seen on the Twigs.
We got over into a field to
avoid some cows – people
working & a few primroses
by the roadside, woodsorr
flowers, the anemone, scentless violets, strawb & th
starry yellow flower which
C calls pile wort. When we
were in the woods beyond
Gowbarrow park we saw a
few daffodils close to the w
side, we fancied that the
lake had floated the seed
ashore & that the
little colony had so sprun
up – But as we went along
there were more & yet mor

4. Dorothy Wordsworth, journal entry of 15 April 1802.

t at last under the boughs
of the trees we saw that there
was a long belt of them
along the
shore about the breadth
of a country turnpike road.
I never saw daffodils so
beautiful they grew among
the mossy stones about & about
them, some rested their heads
upon these stones as on a
pillow for weariness & the
rest tossed & reeled & danced
& seemed as if they verily
laughed with the wind that blew upon them over the lake they
looked so gay ever glancing
This wind blew directly over the lake to them
ever changing ^ There was
here & there a little knot
and a few stragglers a few
yards higher up but they
were so few as not to disturb

Significantly, a more sombre, quiet peace possesses her, soon after William's marriage to Mary Hutchinson; the wild days are over, for better or worse, and from now on she will have to share William, or steal him away:

> October 30th, 1802. William is gone to Keswick. Mary went with him to the top of the Rays. She is returned, and is now sitting near me by the fire. It is a breathless, grey day, that leaves the goldenwoods of autumn quiet in their own tranquility, stately and beautiful in their decaying; the lake is a perfect mirror.

And a perfect mirror of more than the woods and skies.

The Wordsworths led a deliberately retired life, moving by only a margin of miles as their family and income expanded, returning home from their excursions with delight; they died where they had lived. Not so their friend Coleridge, who saw himself as a restless wanderer, too soon transplanted, 'a tree with leaf of feeble stem'. He too was born in a small country town, Ottery St Mary in Devon, but unlike Wordsworth never felt rooted in security – partly, he maintains, because he was sent to school in London after his father's death when he was only ten years old. While the orphaned Wordsworth was happily lodged with a motherly dame in Hawkshead, enjoying such boyish pursuits as riding, skating, fishing and playing cards by the peat fire of the cottage, Coleridge was precociously frequenting London taverns, coffee-houses and bookshops, far from the 'beauteous forms or grand' that enlarged his friend's sympathies.

Wordsworth says, with reason, that he was himself

> Much favoured in my birthplace, and no less
> In that beloved Vale, to which, ere long
> I was transplanted.

Coleridge's transplant was less happy, and throughout his life he was perplexed by a sense of rootlessness, blaming himself and his early years for the ease with which he was deceived by 'false and fair-foliaged tempters', for the rashness with which he chased 'chance-started friendships'.

Coleridge's fame as a poet does not rest on his landscapes, though it is perhaps significant that his finest descriptive work is of his native West Country, in such poems as 'This Lime Tree Bower my Prison', 'The Nightingale', and 'Frost at Midnight'. These, written at Nether Stowey between 1797 and 1799, in the early years of friendship with Wordsworth, show him at his most happily responsive to the natural world, and appear more deeply felt than later effusions on Skiddaw and Saddleback. The landscapes of childhood remain nearest the heart. Like Wordsworth, he believed in the power of the environment and early association, though he was much more given to expounding his faith in terms of philosophic theory, quoting Locke, Hume, Berkeley, Godwin and David Hartley in his support. In some of his poems we see him putting this faith into practice. In 'The Nightingale' he tells us that his infant son Hartley (named after the philosopher) 'knows well the evening star', and that he once soothed the baby's crying by taking him out to the orchard to show him the moon. He has a touching faith that Hartley will grow up more happily than he did, and writes, in 'Frost at Midnight':

> My babe so beautiful! it thrills my heart
> With tender gladness, thus to look at thee,
> And think that thou shall learn far other lore,
> And in far other scenes! For I was reared
> In the great city, pent 'mid cloisters dim,
> And saw nought lovely but the sky and stars.
> But *thou,* my babe! shalt wander like a breeze
> By lakes and sandy shores, beneath the crags
> Of ancient mountain, and beneath the clouds ...
> Therefore all seasons shall be sweet to thee,
> Whether the summer clothe the general earth
> With greenness, or the redbreast sit and sing
> Betwixt the tufts of snow on the bare branch
> Of mossy apple-tree, while the nigh thatch
> Smokes in the sun-thaw; whether the eave-drops fall
> Heard only in the trances of the blast,
> Or if the secret ministry of frost
> Shall hang them up in silent icicles,
> Quietly shining to the quiet Moon.

This hope, alas, was not to be fulfilled: the idyll of thatched cottage with roses peeping through the window and jasmines twining round the porch was not to last. (The cottage, in fact, was plagued with mice, because Coleridge, true to his principles, thought it cruel to set traps.) Coleridge's marriage was unhappy, and he found family life increasingly difficult. Eventually he followed Wordsworth up to the Lakes, and settled his wife at Keswick, where she was shortly joined by the Southeys, but he himself remained a wanderer, tempted by other scenes – by London, and the dreaming opium towers and palaces of Xanadu. There is much pathos in his optimistic letter to his friend Godwin, before the departure for Greta Hall:

> if I cannot procure a suitable house at Stowey I return to Cumberland and settle at Keswick, in a house of such prospect, that if, according to you and Hume, impressions and ideas *constitute* our being, I shall have a tendency to become a god, so sublime and beautiful will be the series of my visual existence ...

When established there in 1800 he wrote proudly, 'I question if there be a room in England which commands a view of mountains, and lakes, and woods and vales superior to that in which I am now sitting.' But it was too late for the mountains and lakes to gain ascendancy over Coleridge's established mental habits; the greatest poem he wrote in the Lake District was fittingly called 'Dejection', and it was in part an analysis of his own self-destructive tendencies. His response to the district described in his *Tour in the Lake Country, 1802*, is enthusiastic enough – indeed, perhaps too enthusiastic. There is little of the settled quiet of his friend's response or of his own West Country days; it is all exclamation marks, wonder, dizziness. Writing

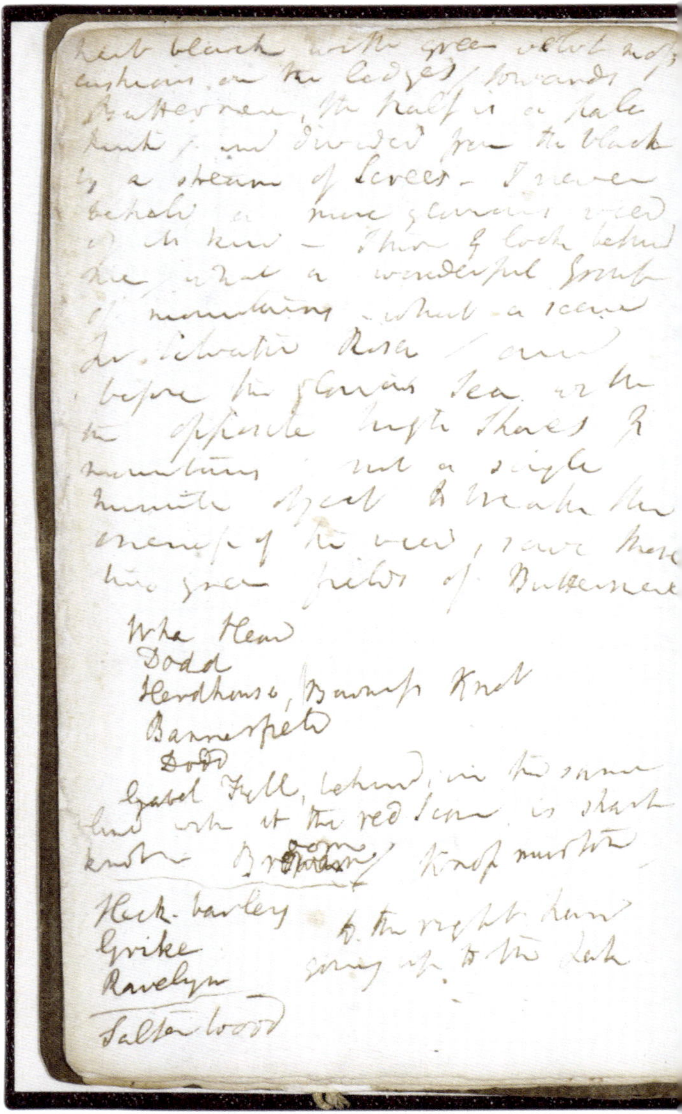

5. Samuel Taylor Coleridge, sketch map of the Lake District, in his notebook of 1802.

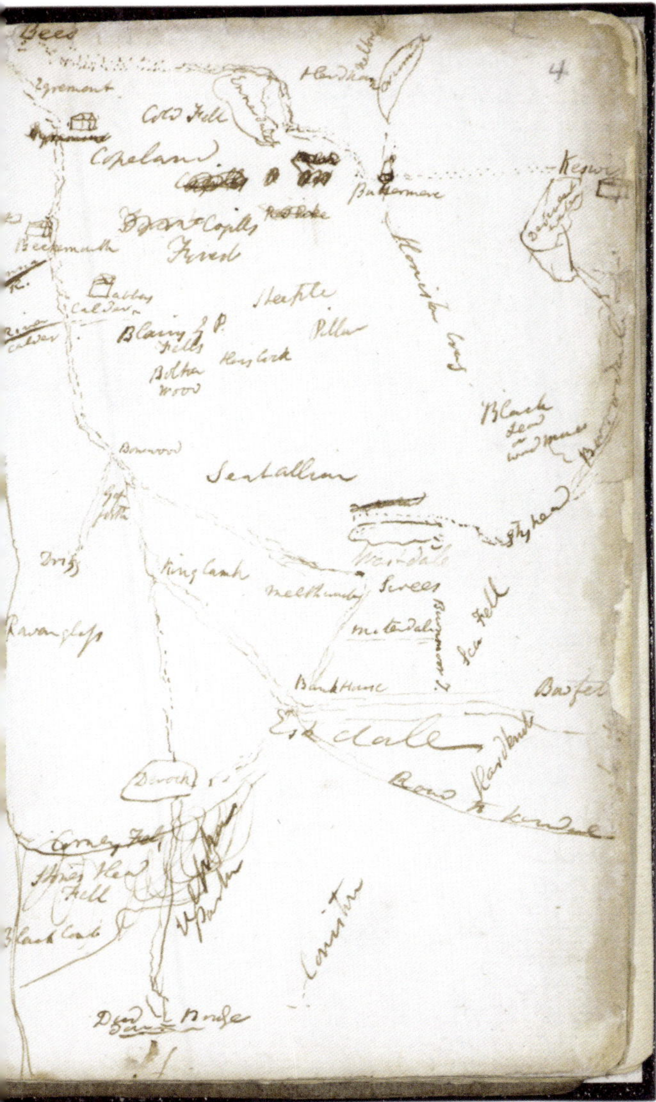
4
Egremont
Cold Fell
Copeland
Buttermere
Calder
Steeple
Pillar
Wastdale
Screes
Sca Fell
Bowfel
Eskdale
Bank House
Devock
Coniston

on the top of Scafell he notes: ‘O! what a look down just under my feet! The frightfullest Cove that might ever be seen, huge perpendicular Precipices, and one Sheep upon its only Ledge …’ And the language in which he writes of the waterfall of Moss Force on Buttermere is as turbulent as its subject:

> The third and highest (of the waterfalls) is a mighty one indeed. It is twice the height of both the others added together, nearly as high as Scale Force, but it rushes down an inclined Plane, and does not fall, like Scale Force; however, if the Plane had been smooth, it is so near a Perpendicular, that it would have appeared to fall, but it is indeed so fearfully savage, and black, and jagged, that it tears the flood to pieces … What a sight it is to look down on such a Cataract! The wheels, that circumvolve it, the leaping up and plunging forward of that infinity of Pearls and Glass Bulbs, the continual change of the Matter, the perpetual Sameness of the Form – it is an awful Image and Shadow of God and the World.

Coleridge’s most impressive landscapes are not English at all: they are the lurid imaginary seascapes of ‘The Rime of the Ancient Marinero, the deep romantic chasms and cedarn covers of an ambiguously Oriental Xanadu. Similarly, the finest descriptive writing of two second generation Romantics, Byron and Shelley, describes not their native land, but their chosen land of exile, Italy. Shelley spent his boyhood in the countryside of West Sussex, and lived in England for more than twenty of his thirty years, but his skylark sang near Leghorn, and his 'Ode to the West Wind' was composed near Florence. The place names that he added to our literature are grand and Romantic enough – Mont Blanc, the Apennines, the Euganean Hills, Naples, Hellas – but they are foreign. Most of his English poems are political, and savage. Leafing through his *Collected Works*, I hoped I had discovered an exception, when I came across 'A Summer Evening Churchyard, Lechlade, Gloucestershire'. This seemed a precise enough location, and was written when he, Peacock, Mary Godwin and Charles Clairmont were on a boating trip in 1815. Alas, the poem is just another disembodied dirge, full of abstract personifications and Gothic horrors – the dusky braids of evening, the mouldering dead in their sepulchres, the awful hush of darkness – and there is nothing to differentiate Lechlade church from any other, apart from one phrase – 'the dry church-tower grass' – which sounds as though it were drawn from observation. One poem, 'The Question', written in 1820, seems to evoke (although in dream) a memory of England:

> And nearer to the river's trembling edge
> There grew broad flag-flowers, purple
> pranked with white,
> And starry river-buds among the sedge,
> And floating water-lilies, broad and bright,
>
> Which lit the oak that overhung the hedge
> With moonlit beams of their own watery light;

> And bulrushes, and reeds of such deep green
> As soothed the dazzled eye with sober sheen ...

But these, as he says, are 'visionary flowers'. The absence of English beauty in his poetry is not accidental: writing, again in 1820, his 'Letter to Maria Gisborne', he describes 'the chaos of green leaves and fruit', the unsickled corn and fireflies of Italy, contrasting them with the London he has left:

> But what see you beside? – a shabby stand
> Of Hackney coaches – a brick house or wall
> Fencing some lonely court, white with the scrawl
> Of our unhappy politics ...

He did not leave England for nothing.

Byron was equally neglectful of home-grown charms, in his poetry at least. Not many Romantic poets are lucky enough to have a converted twelfth-century Augustinian priory for an ancestral home, and its decaying Gothic splendours must have affected his imagination: however, apart from a passage in *Don Juan*, and a few lines of farewell to Newstead Abbey's windy battlements and 'once smiling garden', now choked with hemlock and thistle, he seems for the most part to have cried with his wandering Childe Harold:

> Welcome, ye deserts and ye caves,
> My native land, Good Night!

Athens, Rome, Venice, Seville, the Isles of Greece – he sang of anywhere but home. He made an exception of Scotland, familiar from his childhood years in Aberdeen, writing with nostalgia of the days when his cap was the bonnet, his cloak was the plaid: five stanzas celebrate Lochnagar, 'one of the most sublime and picturesque amongst our Caledonian Alps', but he manages to turn his praise for its foaming cataracts and pine-covered glades into an attack on the England that had treated him, he felt, so badly:

> Years have rolled on, Loch na Garr, since I left you,
> Years must elapse ere I tread you again:
> Nature of verdure and flowers has bereft you
> Yet still are you dearer than Albion's plain.
> England! thy beauties are tame and domestic
> To one who has roved o'er the mountains afar;
> Oh! for the crags that are wild and majestic!
> The steep frowning glories of dark Loch na Garr.

But Byron only played at being a Scottish patriot, donning the theatrical costume and remembering his Scottish ancestry when it suited him. It was Sir Walter Scott who made familiar the Romantic glories of Scottish scenery and Scottish history.

Walter Scott was born in 1771, a year after Wordsworth. His novels and poems now gather dust in second-hand bookshops, and are reprinted largely for the benefit of Scottish universities, but his legend and some of his stories live on (with a strange after-life in Hollywood film and

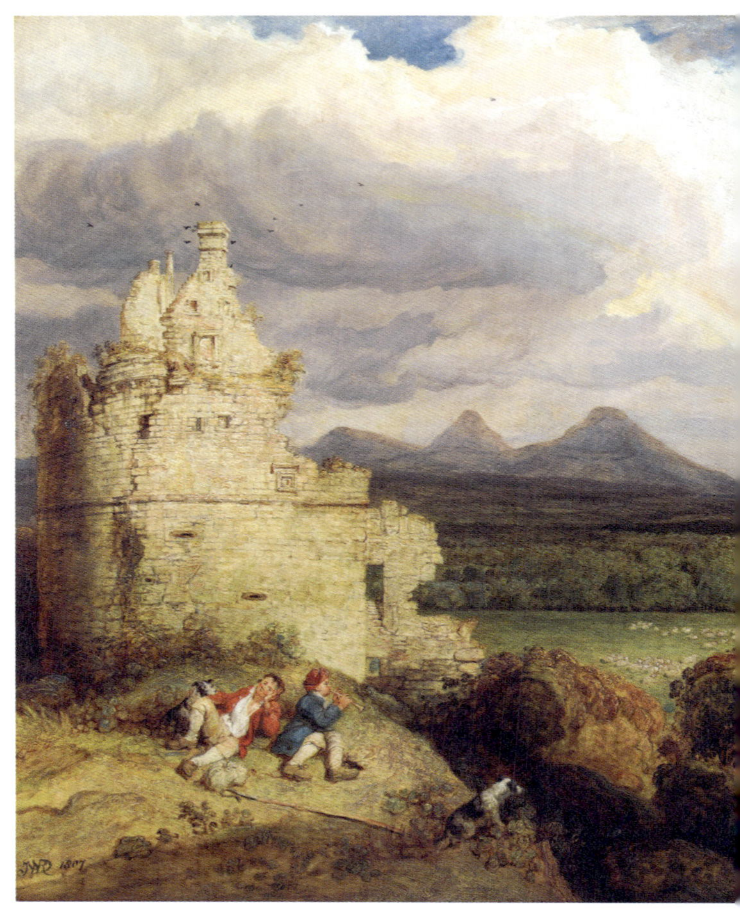

6. James Ward, *The Eildon Hills and The Tweed*, 1807 (reflecting Scott's *The Lay of the Last Minstrel*, 1805). Oil on panel.

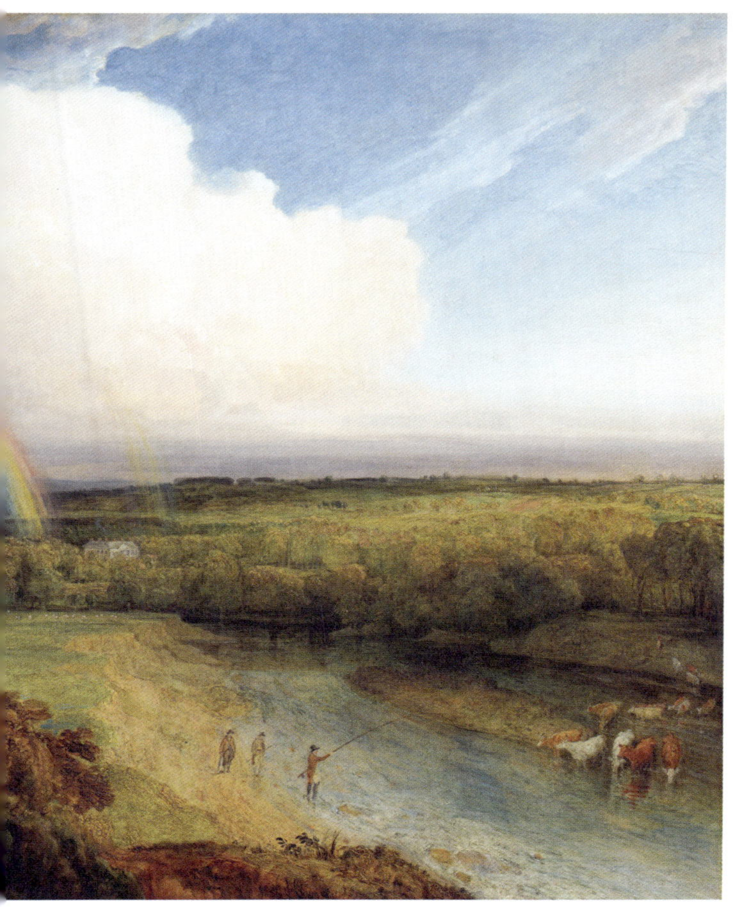

television plots as well as in folklore) and in his day he was far more popular than Wordsworth: Dorothy wrote in 1807 of her brother's new work *The White Doe of Rylstone*, 'I can never expect that poem, or any which he may write, to be immediately popular, like the *Lay of the Last Minstrel* ...' His novels, which appeared at first anonymously, earned him many admiring titles: he was the Wizard of the North, the Great Unknown, the Scottish Prospero. The French idolized him, and he had an immense influence on the work of Balzac. John Hayden, in his introduction to *Scott's Critical Heritage*, states boldly, 'No writer before had been so well received by his contemporaries – *ever*.' His influence was incalculable, and amongst other achievements, he did for Scotland what Wordsworth had done for the Lakes: he praised her beauties, created a new vision, and encouraged the tourist trade. He also restored his country's history and dignity. As we have seen, Dr Johnson considered Scotland quaint and barbaric, its landscapes monotonous, its people and its scenery in decline. Burns, whose grave was already a place of pilgrimage by the time the Wordsworths toured the country in 1803, had provided some excuse for those who wished to see the Scots nation as a nation of picturesque but feckless drunkards: his poetry has been admired but his cult deplored by most patriots. Scott set himself the task of recovering his nation's faith in itself, of rewriting and rediscovering her past. His diligence, his intellectual energy and his success were enormous.

Like Wordsworth, he was fortunate in the scenery of his childhood, and faithful to it. He was brought up in the

Border country, and was to celebrate Tweed and Teviot, Kelso and Liddesdale, the Eildons and the Lammermuirs, Ettrick Forest and St Mary's Loch, in many a rhyme and story. He was familiar with the countryside from his earliest years: as a little boy at his grandfather's farm at Sandy Knowe he would spend days on the hills with the shepherd, watching the flock, the kestrels and the curlews. One day, according to Carole Oman's biography, when a storm came on he was left on the hillside, forgotten, and 'his auntie came running to fetch him home. She found him lying on his back amongst the knolls, clapping his hands at the lightning and crying at every fresh flash, "Bonny! Bonny!"' Such enthusiasm for the wilder aspects of nature remained with him, and infected many a Victorian armchair traveller.

His first major literary work was a collection of carefully restored border ballads, *Minstrelsy of the Scottish Border*. It proved an instant success; so did the *Lay of the Last Minstrel*, in 1805, which drew admiration from both Pitt and Fox, as well as from the Wordsworths, who were treated to a pre-publication reading on their first meeting. Its fame was such that Constable offered him £1,000 for his next work, *Marmion*, without seeing a word of it. This appeared in 1808, to widespread acclaim, both for its romantic and patriotic tale and for its fine landscapes, which included Bamburgh, Whitby, Lindisfarne, Flodden and Loch Skene, amongst many others.

The Lady of the Lake was an even more sensational success, and caused a rush of tourists to Loch Katrine and the Trossachs; a hotel had to be built at Callander for visitors to Ellen's Isle. George Gilfillan, the diligent Victorian editor, wrote in his *Memoir* in 1857,

> 1810 was one of Scott's brightest years. The Lady of the Lake appeared in May, and was received with boundless enthusiasm. Critics vied with each other in eulogiums. On all the roads leading to the Trossachs was suddenly heard the rushing of many chariots and horsemen. Inns were crowded to suffocation. Post-hire permanently rose. Every corner of that fine gorge was explored, and every foot of that beautiful loch was traversed by travellers carrying copies of the book in their hands, or, as they sailed round Ellen's Isle, or climbed the gray scalp of Ben An, or sate in the shady hollow of Coirnanuriskin, or leaned over the still waters of Loch Achray, repeating passages from it with unfeigned rapture. He had hit the public between wind and water. It was as if a ray from heaven had fallen on and revealed a nook of matchless loveliness, and all rejoiced in the gleam and in its revelation.

The days when Dr Johnson could complain that the roads of Scotland afford 'little diversion to the traveller, who seldom sees himself either encountered or overtaken' were over: the age of Bed and Breakfast and crowded caravan sites was on its way.

Scott's novels followed the poems, and added a vast array of ruined abbeys, castles, lochs, mountains and views to the common literary store. He covered the country from coast to coast, including Orkney and the Hebrides, venturing over the border to include Rokeby and Kenilworth, Ditchley, Warwick and York, and a score of other historic sites, on which his comments are quoted in most modern guide books. Like the poems, the novels were read with passionate enthusiasm, and the heroines of later novels pay their debt to their originator. George Eliot's Mary Garth and Maggie Tulliver are both addicts, like George Eliot herself, who did the Scott tour in 1846, visiting Loch Katrine, Melrose and Abbotsford. The Brontës admired and imitated; Emily chose Sir Walter and his protégé James Hogg, the Ettrick Shepherd, as Chief Men for her imaginary childhood games, and Charlotte's happiness when she visited Edinburgh in 1850 is clearly Scott-inspired, as she wrote in a letter to W. S. Williams:

> My dear Sir, do not think I blaspheme when I tell you that your great London town, as compared to Dun-Edin (mine own romantic town), is as prose compared to poetry ... You have nothing like Scott's monument or if you had that and all the glories of architecture, assembled together, you have nothing like Arthur's Seat, and above all you have not the Scotch national character ...

In another letter, she writes 'Melrose and Abbotsford, the very names possess music and magic'.

Thomas Love Peacock, Jane Austen, Dickens, Wellington, Thomas Hardy, Tennyson, Gladstone – the diverse list of admirers is endless. Victoria and Albert both read him, and knew his verses by heart; on their first visit to Scotland in 1842 we find Albert writing, 'There is ... no country where historical traditions are preserved with such fidelity ... Every spot is connected with some interesting historical facts, and with most of those Sir Walter Scott's accurate descriptions have made us familiar.' Sixty years earlier, Dr Johnson had found the Scots lacking, precisely, in historical tradition and written history: Scott had achieved a one-man revolution of attitude. Victoria fell in love with Scotland at first sight, enthused over Edinburgh, quoted *The Lady of the Lake* in her *Journal* when recording her visit to Loch Muich in 1850, and carried the poem with her as a guidebook when she did her tour of the Trossachs and Rob Roy country in 1869. In 1867, when she toured the Borders, she endorsed Scott's advice:

> If thou would'st view fair Melrose aright,
> Go visit it by pale moonlight.

The purchase of Balmoral set the seal of royal approval on Scottish scenery, but Victoria and Albert were looking at the country partly through Scott's eyes: it was he that taught them to praise the beauty of the heather, to prefer the purple hillsides to the Swiss Alps, to find 'solitude, romance and wild loveliness' in what they considered the 'proudest, finest scenery in the world'.

Such descriptive talents were and still are admired: pilgrims still flock to the sites, even though they may not read the novels. But was Scott, in the final judgment, any more than a glorified literary guidebook, a 'picturesque tourist', as Coleridge unkindly called him? Wordsworth, who admired him as a man, was in a sense right to complain (in a letter to R. P. Gillies, 28 April 1815, on *Guy Mannering*) of the 'laborious manner in which everything is placed before your eyes for the production of picturesque effect. When (pictures) are placed upon an easel for the express purpose of being admired, the judicious are apt to take offence.' Many of the set pieces, precise in their roll-call of place names, are dim in outline, as in this extract from *The Lady of the Lake*:

> The noble stag was pausing now,
> Upon the mountain's southern brow,
> Where broad extended, far beneath,
> The varied realms of fair Menteith.
> With anxious eye he wandered o'er
> Mountain and meadow, moss and moor,
> And pondered refuge from his toil
> By far Lochard or Aberfoyle.
> But nearer was the copse-wood gray,
> That waved and wept on Loch-Achray,
> And mingled with the pine-trees blue,
> On the bold cliffs of Ben-venue.

This is incantatory stuff, but as Coleridge wrote to Wordsworth, all you need for this kind of verse is 'a vast string of patronymics, and names of Mountains, Rivers etc.' The novels are much more accurate in their sense of place, but even here, the scenes and set pieces are stage-managed.

Scott's success heralded the golden age of the nineteenth-century novel. He was followed by scores of imitators, many now forgotten, some more distinguished than their model. His painting of everyday country life inspired George Eliot and Elizabeth Gaskell; his sense of place and romantic atmosphere influenced the Brontës, Thomas Hardy and a host of lesser writers. He confirmed that it was unnecessary to look abroad, as the 'Radcliffe school' of Romantic novelists had done: there were stores of undiscovered riches nearer home. Italy and Spain were forgotten, as Cornwall and Cumberland, Yorkshire and Dorset, Devon and Shropshire found their chroniclers.

The Brontë sisters have always been rightly identified with their Yorkshire home. Their genius flourished in isolation. Their lonely childhood at Haworth parsonage and their rambles on the surrounding moors formed their characters and their work. For Emily in particular, place was more important than people. There was nothing of the tourist in her: she left home rarely and reluctantly, and when away she fell ill pining for the heather and harebells and familiar sights of Haworth. Her landscapes are among the finest in the language, and all of them are drawn from her own immediate and narrow experience. Unlike Scott's, they are never posed, never picturesque, never held up for admiration. They are an integral part of the book. The characters of *Wuthering Heights* grow out of its scenery as naturally as the trees and rocks themselves. Emily constantly sees and describes people in terms of landscape: in her famous outburst to Nelly Dean, Catherine exclaims, 'My love for Linton is like the foliage in the woods. Time will change it, I'm well aware, as winter changes the trees. My love for Heathcliff resembles the eternal rocks beneath – a source of little visible delight, but necessary.' After her death, Heathcliff says, 'I cannot look down to this floor, but her features are shaped on the flags! In every cloud, in every tree – filling the air at night, and caught by glimpses in every object, by day I am surrounded with her image!' Nelly describes her daughter's face as being 'just like the landscape – shadows and sunshine flitting over it, in rapid succession ...' This insistence is more than a literary device: it shows a sense of the affinity of man and nature so profound that many have described Emily as a mystic.

Yet there is hardly a set description in the whole novel. The overpowering physical reality of its world is built up from a hundred small natural touches, each revealing some character trait or making some dramatic point, or providing a turning point in the action. The exposed situation of the Heights is part of Emily's plot: in the second chapter the narrator Lockwood looks out of the window 'to examine the weather. A sorrowful sight I saw: dark night coming down prematurely, and sky and hill mingled in one whirl of suffocating snow.' Only a few phrases, and we see the snowstorm through Lockwood's apprehensive eyes: it is this storm that imprisons him for the night at the Heights, and provides the pretext for the whole story.

Slowly, with unobtrusive details, Emily Brontë builds up the contrast between the old farmhouse with its stunted firs, gaunt thorns and rough-spoken inhabitants, and Thrushcross Grange, with its pleasant park, its sheltering

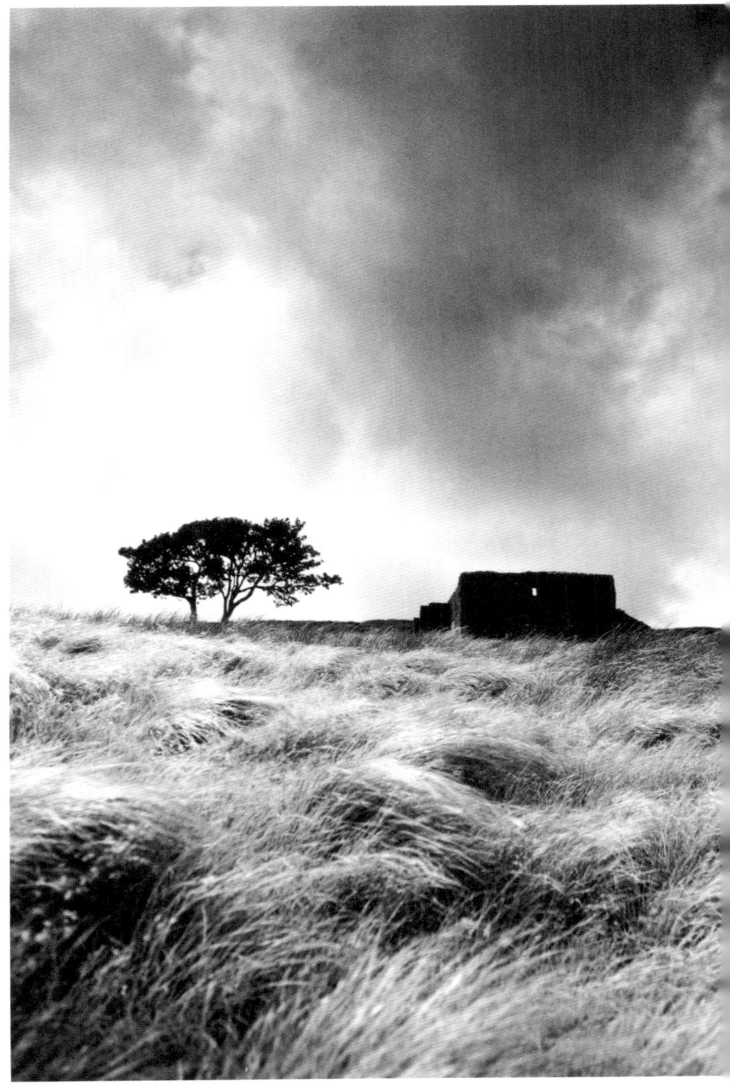

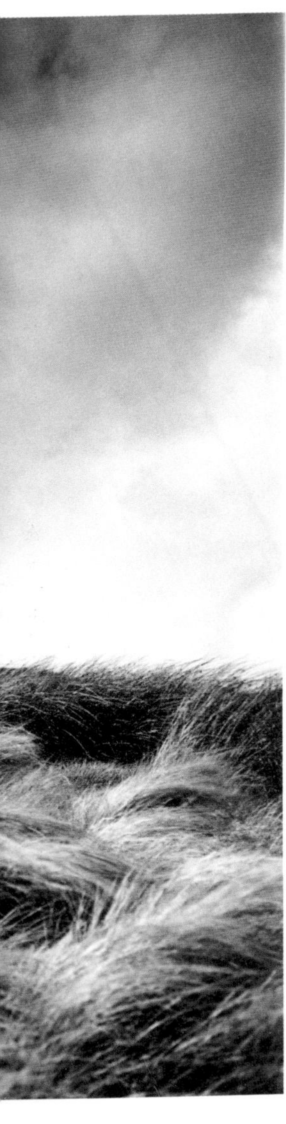

7. Fay Godwin, Top Withens, near Haworth, Yorkshire, 1977

fences and plantations, its summer murmur of foliage, its orchard of apples; a contrast which, again, *is* the plot, for Catherine has to choose between the two representatives of these places, and is doomed for choosing wrongly. The book has a fine variety: although we tend to think of the tempestuous and gloomy scenes first, the mood is by no means always dark, nor is the tone indulgently romantic. The gloom is balanced by the tone of Nelly Dean, perceptive yet matter-of-fact, a country woman who knows the goings-on of earth and sky. Nelly's comments are always both accurate and evocative: 'It was a close, sultry day: devoid of sunshine, but with a sky too dappled and hazy to threaten rain ...' There are more enthusiastic raptures about the beauties of nature in Jane Austen than in Emily Brontë, the only possible exception being the dreams of young Catherine and Linton, in Chapter 24:

> He said the pleasantest manner of spending a hot July day was lying from morning till evening on a bank of heath in the middle of the moors with the bees humming dreamily about among the bloom, and the larks singing high up over head ... mine was rocking in a rustling green tree, with a west wind blowing, and bright, white clouds flitting rapidly above; and not only larks, but throstles, and blackbirds, and linnets, and cuckoos pouring out music on every side, and the moors seen at a distance, broken into cool, dusky dells; but close by great swells of long grass undulating in waves to the breeze; and woods and sounding water, and the whole world awake and wild

> with joy. He wanted all to lie in an ecstasy of peace:
> I wanted all to sparkle and dance in a glorious jubilee.

But Catherine and Linton are still children: they soon learn better.w

Visitors to Haworth will not be surprised to find that Emily, whose home overlooks the graveyard, writes with an easy familiarity of death and gravestones. Perhaps she played among them, as did Catherine and Heathcliff. There is no element of Gothic extravagance in her use of graves and burials: even Heathcliff's embracing of Catherine's corpse seems in a different tradition from its literary predecessors. It is a real world that she draws, with its changing seasons, a world where the bleak winds and bitter northern skies give way to summer, as Lockwood finds on his return after nearly a year's absence (Chapter 32):

> The grey churchyard looked greyer, and the lonely churchyard lonelier. I distinguished a moor sheep cropping turf on the graves. It was sweet, warm weather – too warm for travelling; but the heat did not hinder me from enjoying the delightful scenery above and below: had I seen it nearer August, I'm sure it would have tempted me to waste a month among its solitudes. In winter nothing more dreary, in summer nothing more divine, than those glens shut in by hills, and those bluff, bold swells of heath.

Emily's poetry is similarly imbued with her feeling for purple heather bells, storm-worn walls, skyscapes, storms, and warm summer afternoons. To her, Haworth was no prison, for, as she writes in 'Often Rebuked, yet always back Returning', the path to the moors that leads away from the parsonage leads to freedom unlimited:

I'll walk where my own nature would be leading:
It vexes me to choose another guide:
Where the grey flocks in ferny glades are feeding;
Where the wild wind blows on the mountain side.

What have those lonely mountains worth revealing?
More glory and more grief than I can tell:
The earth that wakes *one* human heart to feeling
Can centre both the worlds of Heaven and Hell.

Her sisters, Charlotte and Anne, were not so content with their solitary lives; Charlotte in particular yearned to travel, and her descriptions of Brussels show a more heightened excitement than her Yorkshire novel, *Shirley*. On the first page, she claims *Shirley* will be as 'unromantic as Monday morning', and makes visible efforts to check and counterbalance her own poetic impulses, reminding us, as Emily does not, that Yorkshire was already a county of flourishing industry, and that if one walked in the other direction from Haworth one reached not the moors but the mills of Keighley, and its Mechanics' Institute Library. Yet there is something Romantic in her appreciation of the industrial landscape. The unpoetic curate Malone, 'not given to close observation of Nature', fails to notice the drama of the sky – 'a muffled, streaming vault, all black, save where, towards the east, the furnaces of Stillbro' ironworks threw a tremulous lurid shimmer on the horizon' – but Charlotte is highly responsive. Charlotte mocks Shirley's suitor, Sir Philip, for his 'literary turn', which expresses itself in moonlight walks, reading long ballads, and seeking sequestered rustic seats, and tries hard to reconcile herself to a more practical vision of man's relation to landscape: in the last chapter, 'The Winding-Up', we find industrialist Robert Moore telling the romantic Caroline of the changes he plans in these terms:

> '... I can double the value of their mill-property: I can line yon barren Hollow with lines of cottages, and rows of cottage-gardens –'
>
> 'Robert? And root up the copse?'
>
> 'The copse shall be firewood ere five years elapse: the beautiful wild ravine shall be a smooth descent; the green natural terrace shall be a paved street: there shall be cottages in the dark ravine, and cottages on the lonely slopes: the rough pebbled track shall be an even, firm, broad, black, sooty road, bedded with cinders from my mill: and my mill, Caroline – my mill shall fill its present yard.'
>
> 'Horrible! You will change our blue hill-country air into the Stillboro' smoke atmosphere.'
>
> 'I will pour the waters of Pactolus through the valley of Briarfield.'
>
> 'I like the beck a thousand times better.'
>
> 'I will get an act for enclosing Nunnely Common, and parcelling it out into farms.'

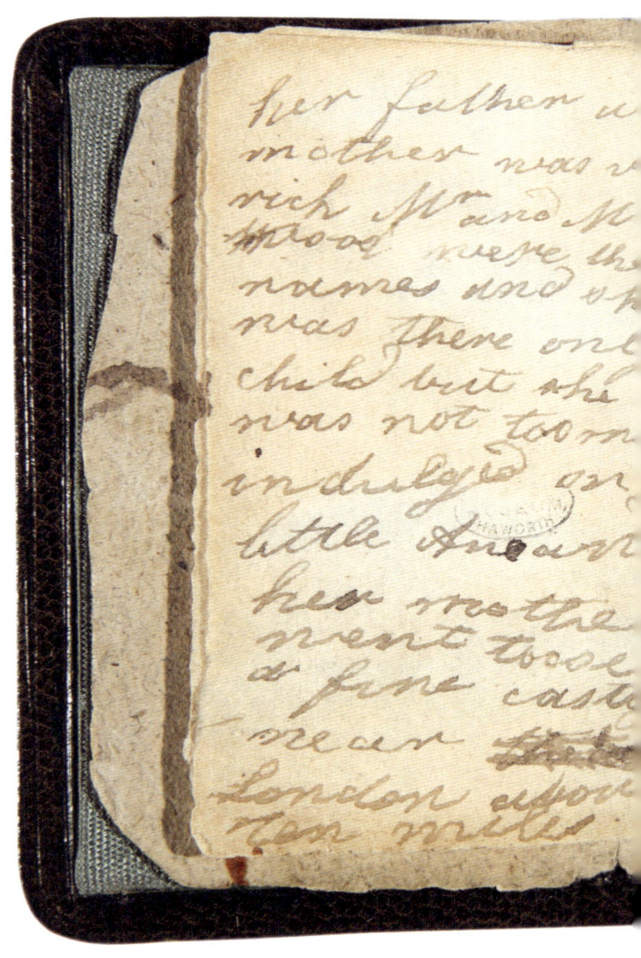

her father w
mother was r
rich Mr and M
Wood were th
names and o
was there onl
child but she
was not too m
indulged an
little
her mothe
went too se
a fine castl
near
London abou
ten miles

8. Charlotte Brontë, 'There once was a little girl, and her name was Ane', miniature manuscript with watercolour drawings of a seascape and a woman out walking, 1828.

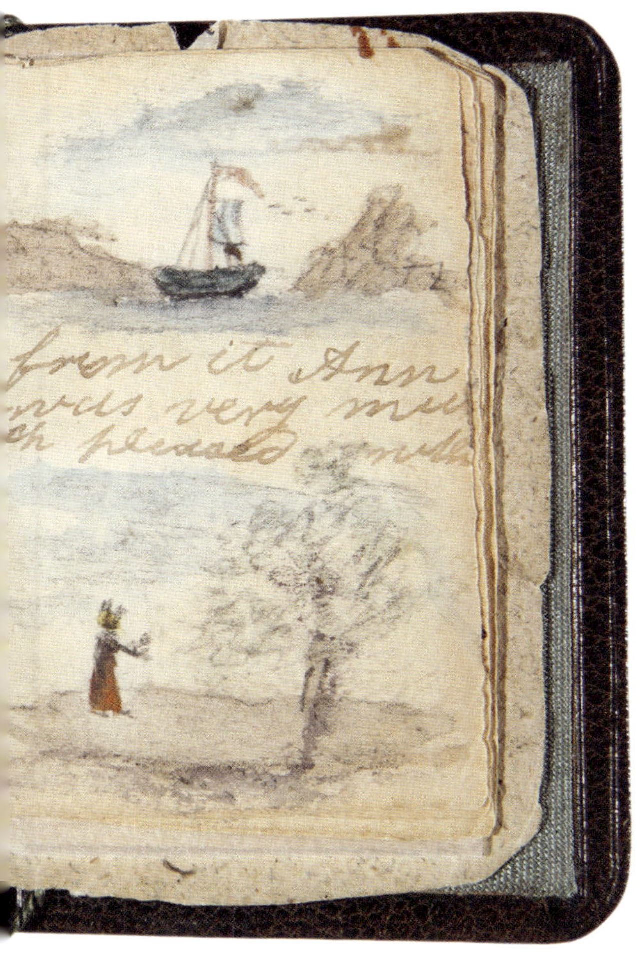
from it Ann
very
pleased

> 'Stillboro' Moor, however, defies you, thank Heaven! What can you grow in Bilberry Moss? What will flourish on Rushedge?'

Here Charlotte accurately foretells the future of the landscape, and the days, not too far distant, when only the wildest and most resistant regions would defy man. Moore clearly suspects that the National Parks and 'areas of outstanding natural beauty' that the future would learn to protect would simply prove to be areas that were not worth exploiting. He is on the side of Jane Austen's sensible heroes, preferring the useful to the Picturesque – yet with how much more sinister a warning than Jane Austen could deliver, a warning of pollution and spreading industrial estates, instead of a dream of neat and prosperous farming.

Charlotte sees both sides: her heart is with Caroline, but she is ashamed to appear in the already conventional role of the soft-hearted, soft-headed, girlish 'nature lover'. More self-conscious, and therefore more self-critical than Emily, she is more aware of the traps of romance and romantic fiction. Yet she too could respond at times with a violence that made her speechless. There is something deeply moving in the account of her first sight of the sea, at Bridlington, in 1839. She went with her prosaic friend Ellen Nussey, who later wrote that Charlotte was so overpowered by the scene that 'she could not speak till she had shed some tears'. She signalled to Ellen to move on, to leave her to experience the fulfillment of her intense anticipation alone. When Ellen returned, 'her eyes were red and swollen, she was still trembling', and for the rest of the day she remained subdued and exhausted. Years later, this scene was repeated, when she visited Ireland with her husband Mr Nicholls: he too had to withdraw tactfully as she admired the wild foam of the Atlantic and its rocky 'iron-bound' coast at Kilkee.

Anne too loved the sea, which she first saw at Scarborough, a few miles north of Bridlington; she was working as a governess at the time, and suffering from deep depression. The sea revived her, and she conveyed her gratitude in both her novels. Her heroine Agnes Grey chooses Scarborough as the location for her little school, in the novel's poignantly happy ending:

> There was a feeling of freshness and vigour in the very streets, and when I got free of the town, when my foot was on the sands and my face towards the broad, bright bay, no language can describe the effect of the deep, clear azure of the sky and ocean, the bright morning sunshine on the semi-circular barrier of craggy cliffs surmounted by green swelling hills, and on the smooth, wide sands, and the low rocks out at sea – looking, with their clothing of weeds and moss, like little grass-grown islands – and above all, on the brilliant, sparkling waves. And then the unspeakable purity and freshness of the air!

Anne herself was less fortunate: she went to die there at the age of twenty-nine, in Charlotte's words 'where she would be happiest', and passed away at two o'clock on a cloudless afternoon, sitting in an armchair, gazing at the view she loved so well. The distressed doctor wondered at 'her fixed tranquillity of spirit.' Nature proved kind to Anne, but little else in her life did.

The Brontë lives and landscapes inspired many tributes, from Matthew Arnold's moving elegy, 'Haworth Churchyard', written after Charlotte's death in 1855, to Sylvia Plath's 'Wuthering Heights', published in 1971. Arnold's Haworth is mournfully accurate, catching both the industrial and romantic aspects of the region:

> Where, behind Keighley, the road,
> Up to the heart of the moors
> Between heath-clad showery hills
> Runs, and colliers' carts
> Poach the deep ways coming down,
> And a rough, grimed race have their homes –
> There on its slope is built
> The moorland town. But the church
> Stands on the crest of the hill,
> Lonely and bleak; – at its side
> The parsonage-house and the graves.

Elizabeth Gaskell's famous life of Charlotte has some finely evocative descriptions of the district, and on her first visit she wrote to a friend, 'The wind goes piping and wailing and sobbing round the square, unsheltered house in a very strange, unearthly way', revealing herself as an impressionable visitor, like Lockwood at the Heights. Plath too paid tribute to the tragedy in the countryside;

she writes of the sheep, the pale skies, the tilted horizons, the pouring wind that flattens everything. One tragic poet writing of another, she says:

> If I pay the roots of the heather
> Too close attention, they will invite me
> To whiten my bones among them.

As the nineteenth century progressed, other regions found their poets and their novelists. It was inevitable, perhaps, that Exmoor would produce its *Lorna Doone*, *Westward Ho!* its Westward Ho! (an inverse relationship, this, for the place was named after Kingsley's novel) – Tintagel its Tennyson and Swinburne, Dorset its Hardy, Cornwall its *Rebecca*, Shropshire its Housman and Mary Webb. The taste for the Romantic became, more generally, a taste for the unspoiled and wild, for the kind of scenery that could resist the growing population and industry of the busy Victorian age. Writers began to sense that wildness might disappear, and appreciated it the more. Far from fearing it, they started up the refrain that Hopkins voiced when he wrote:

> What would the world be, once bereft
> Of wet and of wildness? Let them be left –
> Let them be left. O, wildness and wet;
> Long live the weeds and the wilderness yet.

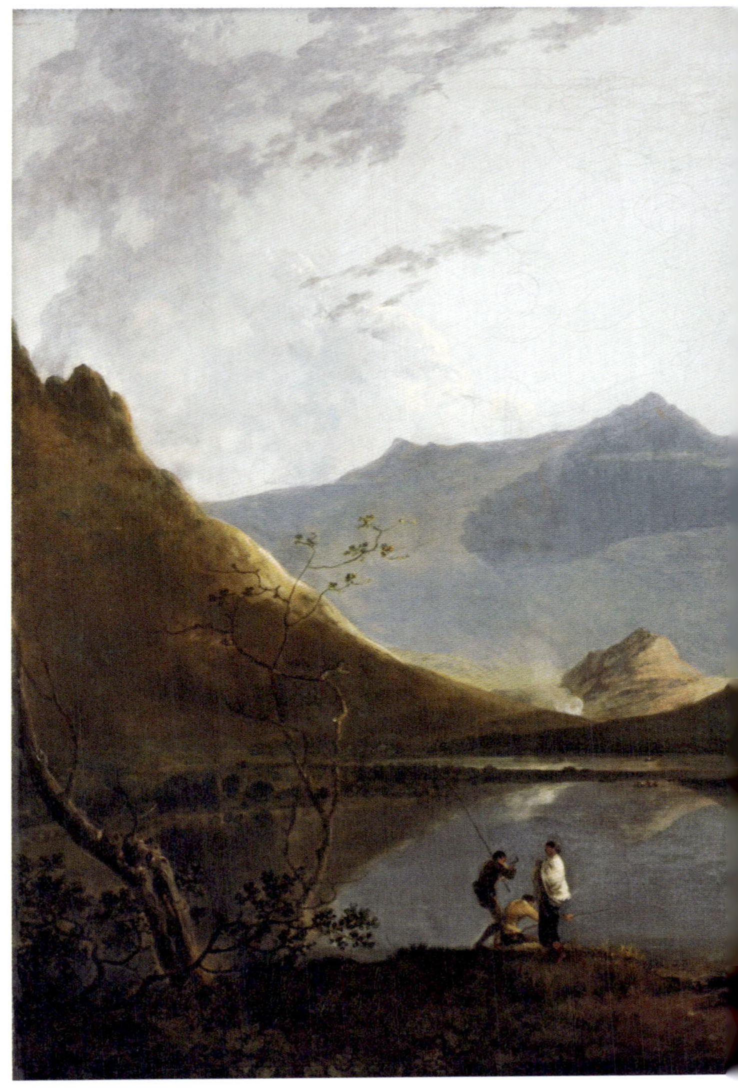

9. Richard Wilson, *Snowdon* [Yr Wyddfa] *from Llyn Nantlle*, 1765–66. Oil on canvas.

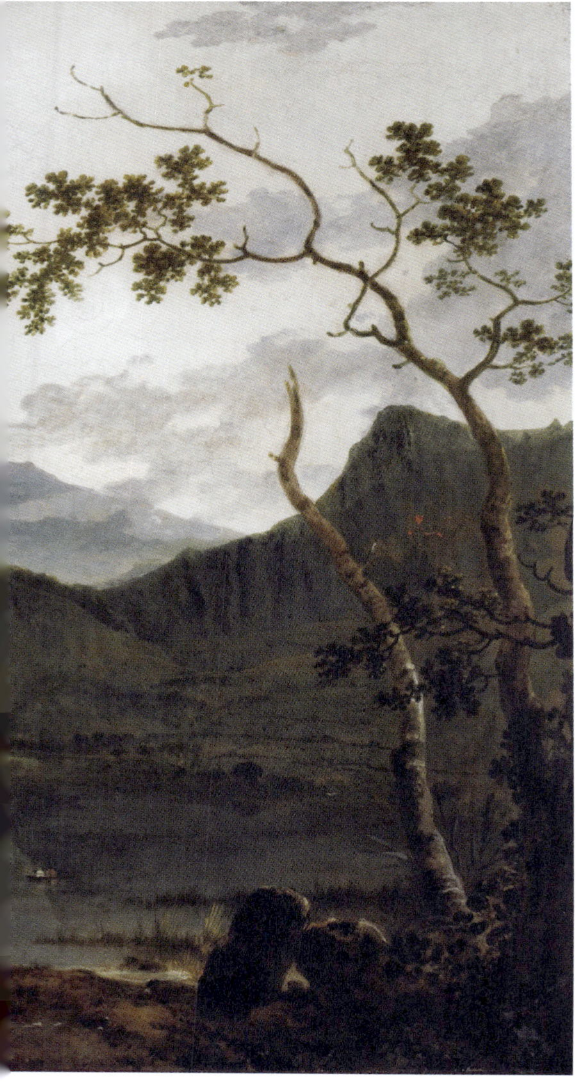

Some regions have become hackneyed shrines of literary pilgrimage; others would seem at first sight to have had less than their share of romantic appreciation. Wales, which is romantic enough, with its wild mountains, its fierce history, its ruined castles and Arthurian legends, produced no Walter Scott, and there are few Welsh novelists of the nineteenth century, though the eighteenth-century artist Richard Wilson, born in the Vale of the Dyfi, declared that 'everything the landscape painter could want was to be found in North Wales'. This apparent lack is probably a tribute to the comparative strength of the indigenous Welsh culture and literature, which remains inaccessible to the ordinary English reader, and which needed no imported enthusiasts. Tourists in their thousands now flock there every year, but they understand little beyond what meets their eyes (though that is certainly worth seeing). George Borrow's classic account, *Wild Wales*, was coldly received when it appeared in 1862, and illustrates the difficulties encountered by the traveller. Borrow, though English born and bred, could speak and read Welsh, and his pilgrimage took him to shrines little visited, some unmarked on any map: as he told one of his many chance acquaintances who asked him why he would not take the railroad, 'I am fond of the beauties of nature; now it is impossible to see much of the beauties of nature unless you walk. I am likewise fond of poetry, and take special delight in inspecting the birthplaces and haunts of poets.' His interest aroused astonishment in the Welsh, unaccustomed to such visitors. Borrow included in his pilgrimage the poets Huw Morris and Goronwy

Owen, the patriot Owen Glendower and his bard, Iolo Goch, quoting from them in appropriate moments – on Snowdon and at Glendower's home at Sycharth, where he dismissed his guide to contemplate the lost past in solitude, and reduced himself, Charlotte Brontë-like, to tears – 'covering my face with my hands, I wept like a child'. Snowdon was to him the Parnassus of Europe, and he describes the view with rapture: from the top he saw 'a scene inexpressibly grand ... Peaks, pinnacles and huge moels stood up here and there, about us and below us, partly in glorious light, partly in deep shade ...'; below them lay 'numerous lakes and lagoons, which, like sheets of ice or polished silver, lay reflecting the rays of the sun in the deep valleys at his feet'. Yet, oddly, one of his most descriptive phrases is one of his least poetic: of the celebrated waterfall of Pistyll Rhaeadr in Denbighshire he wrote that seen from a distance it looked like 'a strip of gray linen hanging over a crag'.

The greatest twentieth-century novelist of Welsh landscape, John Cowper Powys, had a complex relationship with his national identity. Born in Derbyshire, and brought up in the South West of England (about which he wrote great topographical novels, including *A Glastonbury Romance* (1932) and *Weymouth Sands* (1934), he was also deeply conscious of and proud of his ancient Welsh lineage, and of the bardic tradition. He spent the last three decades of his long and intensely creative life in Wales, first in Corwen and then in Blaenau Ffestiniog, in a countryside which inspired two magnificent historical novels, *Owen Glendower* (1940) and *Porius* (1951).

His evocations of the sublimity of Snowdon and Cader Idris and Lake Bala have a Miltonic grandeur, but he also had the keenest eye for the smallest botanical detail, for 'the slippery knots of the exposed roots of heather, the burnished stalks of bracken, the dead blackness of crow-berries, the scaly surface of yellow-green lichens, the orange-pink clumps of stone-crop'. His modest home in Blaenau, not the most conventionally attractive of Welsh towns, became a site of literary pilgrimage for admiring younger writers, who would visit him and his life's companion, Phyllis Plater, and wonder why they had chosen to live so remotely amongst the slate quarries.

Other more obviously romantic sites were more accessible to visitor and writer. Tintagel, acclaimed by Malory and Geoffrey of Monmouth as the birthplace of King Arthur, would have found its poets had the Arthurian legend never settled on it, though, no doubt, the legend helped. The picturesque ruins appear, in fact, to be built on the remains of an earlier Celtic monastery rather than on an Arthurian stronghold, but fact has little to do with it. Malory spares it hardly a descriptive phrase, but this lack the Victorians made good. The Reverend R. S. Hawker, vicar of Morwenstow, claimed the distinction of having introduced Tennyson and Kingsley to the charms of the region, and his own tales of smugglers, shipwrecks and storms, as described in Charles Tennyson's *Life of Tennyson*, show a Byronic pleasure in the grandeur of the elements, as well as a Christian compassion for the victims: 'So cruel is that shore that after a wreck he would send a man with a basket to collect the gobbets of flesh cut from the bodies of the poor sailors by the sharp rocks against which the waves battered them. These ... he would bury with all reverence.' Baring-Gould, in his popular life of Hawker (1876), writes dramatically, 'The coast from Tintagel to Hartland is almost unrivalled for grandeur. The restless Atlantic is ever thundering on this iron-walled coast. The roar can be heard ten miles inland; flakes of foam are picked up after a storm at Holsworthy ...The swell comes unbroken from Labrador to hurl itself against this coast, and to be shivered into foam on its iron cuirass.'

Appreciation of the grandeurs and beauties of the sea was largely a Romantic innovation. In earlier times, not surprisingly, men had tended to associate the sea with peril rather than with beauty. Fear was more powerful than the romance of travel. Houses were built safely inland, and those near the coast were built with their backs to the coast, avoiding a sea view – Seaton Delaval, in Northumberland, is an often-quoted example of this attitude. By the beginning of the nineteenth century, this aversion was beginning to abate, and resorts were developed as holidaymakers learned of the newly proclaimed health-giving properties of sea bathing. Jane Austen in her unfinished *Sanditon* (1817) describes the turning point of the story: the book marks, precisely, the shift from the old eighteenth-century view towards the new Romantic conception of the coast. Mr Parker, who has built a new house by the sea, sings the praises of the grandeur of storms, and presents being rocked in bed by them as a positive pleasure. Sensible Charlotte sees the advantages of his former home, a sheltered snug-looking inland place rich in orchards, meadows and fields. Yet even Charlotte's spirits rise at the prospect of the sea from her bedroom window, dancing and sparkling in sunshine and freshness. The age was on the side of Mr Parker, and resorts were developed all round Britain, inevitably ruining some of the beauty that visitors came to seek, yet creating at the same time some of our more elegant Regency architecture – Brighton, Weymouth, Eastbourne are all products of the new passion. And despite *Sanditon*'s bias, one of Jane Austen's most celebrated moments takes place by the sea: all Austen readers know the scene in *Persuasion* where Louisa Musgrove falls from the Cobb. When Tennyson visited Lyme in 1867, he went at once to call on his friend Palgrave (of *Palgrave's Golden Treasury*) and said 'Now take me to the Cobb and show me where Louisa Musgrove fell.' More recently, John Fowles, who lived for years at Lyme, set some of the most dramatic moments of his popular novel *The French Lieutenant's Woman* in the same location. One might fancy the spirit of the place drew writers to it. The spirit of the place, the spirit of Jane Austen – the two are now intermingled, for any visitor.

The Romantic poets also paid their tribute to the sea. Byron cried in *Childe Harold's Pilgrimage*:

> Roll on, thou deep and dark blue Ocean – roll!
> Ten thousand fleets sweep over thee in vain;
> Man marks the earth with ruin – his control
> Stops with the shore ...

and succeeding generations were to praise the merciless waves, the violence of the elements, in a way that the more sensible eighteenth century would have found ridiculous. Arthur Hugh Clough's stanza,

> On stormy nights when wild north-westers rave,
> How proud a thing to fight with wind and wave!
> The dripping sailor on the reeling mast
> Exults to bear, and scorns to wish it past ...

cannot have found many sympathetic echoes from real mariners. Tennyson has some fine seascapes, some from early recollections of Mablethorpe on the Lincolnshire coast, some from his years at Freshwater on the Isle of Wight, some from his ramblings in Cornwall in pursuit of King Arthur, where his companion Palgrave would infuriate him by running after him calling 'Tennyson! Tennyson!' whenever he strayed too near the edge of a cliff or rock. Yet Tennyson's most famous sea poem,

> Break, break, break
> On thy cold gray stones, O Sea –

was composed in a Lincolnshire lane, many miles inland.

Swinburne also visited Tintagel, and was attracted by the violence of the coast. *Tristram of Lyonesse* is full of descriptions of the sea, of foam-flowers and sea-roses, of the wild wrath of the Cornish foam, of 'wind-hollowed heights and gusty bays'. In a letter to Mary Gordon, 2 September 1864, he writes enthusiastically of Boscastle:

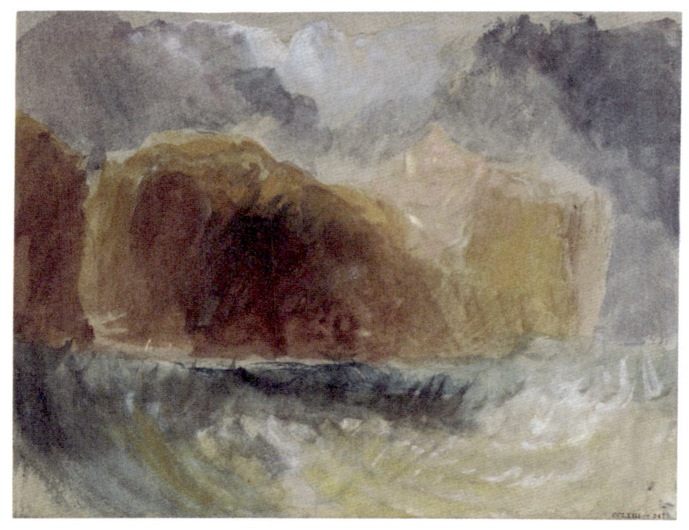

10. J. M. W. Turner, *Tintagel Castle from the Sea*, *c.* 1825. Gouache and watercolour on paper.

> You can imagine how the sea swings to and fro between the cliffs, foams, swells, beats and baffles itself against the steep faces of the rock. I should guess it must be unique in England. Seen from above and on horseback it was very queer, dark grey swollen water, caught as it were in a trap, and heaving with rage against both sides at once, edged with long panting lines of incessant foam that swung and lapped along the deep steep cliffs without breaking, and had not room to roll at ease.

(Not surprisingly, he was so taken by the wild North Sea when staying at Wallington, Newcastle, that he wrote to his friend Richard Monckton Milnes in discreet French expressing his regret that the '*cher et digne*' Marquis de Sade had never imagined '*des supplices de mer*'.)

More peaceably, though more tragically, Keats composed his last sonnet, 'Bright Star!', on board ship off the coast of Dorset, after a day exploring the caves and rock pools at Lulworth: he was on his way to Rome, his last resting place, and his vision of

> The moving waters at their priestlike task
> Of pure ablution round earth's human shores

was his last sight of England.

Matthew Arnold's 'Forsaken Merman' is a fine example of a newly popular genre, the subaqueous landscape. More importantly, 'Dover Beach' is one of the most impressive and moving of Victorian seascapes:

The sea is calm tonight.
The tide is full, the moon lies fair
Upon the straits; – on the French coast the light
Gleams and is gone; the cliffs of England stand,
Glimmering and vast, out in the tranquil bay.
Come to the window, sweet is the night air!
Only, from the long line of spray
Where the sea meets the moon-blanch'd land,
Listen! you hear the grating roar
Of pebbles which the waves draw back, and fling,
At their return, up the high strand,
Begin, and cease, and then again begin,
With tremulous cadence slow, and bring
The eternal note of sadness in ...

Place, sound, mood and thought intermingle marvellously in this poem; Arnold's stoic melancholy as he contemplates the 'long, withdrawing roar' of the Sea of Faith rises with the utmost grace and inevitability from the scene itself. The sea has always provided man with a store of images: much could be written of its changing symbolic significance in the imagination. Coventry Patmore, almost an exact contemporary of Arnold's, was to become a Catholic, finding the faith that Arnold could not intellectually approve. He too uses the sea as an image, in an extremely interesting little poem, '*Magna est Veritas*', as characteristically Victorian as 'Dover Beach':

Here, in this little bay,
Full of tumultuous life and great repose,

Where, twice a day,
The purposeless, glad ocean comes and goes,
Under high cliffs, and far from the huge town,
I sit me down.
For want of me the world's course will not fail:
When all its work is done, the lie shall rot;
The truth is great, and shall prevail,
When none cares whether it prevail or not.

No earlier poem, surely, could so have combined religious faith with an awareness of the insignificance of man and of mankind: the purposeless glad ocean of truth needs no recognition, it was and will be. Man's insignificance is itself insignificant.

Wordsworth, Scott, Byron and the Brontës were romantic but bracing: there is nothing enervating about their landscapes. This was not true of a later generation of poets, over whom crept a mood of listlessness that somehow turned the most turbulent dramas into lotus-eating swoons. While most of this languor can be traced to the increasing irrelevance of 'poesy' in an age when the novel was tackling the more interesting (and picturesque) problems, perhaps a little can be laid at Tennyson's door, and, more specifically, at the door of his birthplace. The effect of Somersby and the Lincolnshire landscape on Tennyson was profound, and through him, on mid- and lateVictorian literature as a whole.

Lincolnshire is a varied county, and Somersby lies in one of its more varied regions. The poet's grandson Charles Tennyson describes it thus:

> Somersby is a tiny hamlet tucked remotely away in a corner of the Lincolnshire wolds, a range of hills reaching here and there a height of five hundred feet. One line of these (then a complete wilderness, untilled and overrun by rabbits) stretches north and south, between the village and the sea, and from it another range goes north-westwards towards Market Rasen and Caister. The old Rectory lies in the angle of the two, about 150 feet above sea level, in a pleasant valley, down which flows the brook that formed the basis of so many of Alfred's similes and descriptions. The slopes of wold and valley are dotted with copses and noble trees, amongst which lie tiny villages and square-towered churches ... Beyond the eastern range of hills lies the marsh, a flat strip of rich pasture land about five to eight miles wide, divided up into fields by broad ditches, which are filled in summer with tall, feathery reeds. Beyond this is the North Sea, peculiar for the long rise and fall of the tide over the flat sandy shore and fringed by a line of high sand dunes on which Alfred loved to wander, feeling as though he were standing 'on the spine bone of the world'.

Through this landscape the poet would wander, as a boy and a young man, sometimes walking all night long, and his poetry is full of impressions of his surroundings. He was very short-sighted, which one might guess from the writing alone, for it is marked by extremely precise, close descriptions – of black ash buds, of flecks of sea foam, of pebbles, of caterpillars – and by huge, vague, misty horizons. The prevailing mood is one of melancholy and heaviness, even in the early poems, before the death of Tennyson's loved friend Arthur Hallam, the inspiration of *In Memoriam*: the characteristically Tennysonian world is one of dying swans, decaying flowers, dark rooks in elm trees, dark wolds, desolate creeks, dim meres, and dew-drenched wood walks. His heroines are the Sleeping Beauty, the Lady of Shalott who can observe the real world only through a mirror, Mariana waiting wearily in her moated grange. The languid atmosphere that breathes from the poems is overwhelming, and it captured the Victorian imagination – partly, perhaps, because it was new, newly formulated, utterly unlike the rugged mountainous scenery of Tennyson's poetic predecessors, and partly because it suited the Victorian mood so well – and, by suiting it, helped to create it.

Many of the poems are set in a specifically Lincolnshire setting, with the sound of the bells of Lincoln Cathedral ringing in the distance, the willows stooping over the river Witham or the lush vegetation of wood and garden in the foreground. *In Memoriam* in particular is a portrait of a much-loved landscape, combining minute detail – the rosy plumelets of the larch, the tulips dashed with fiery dew, the violets blowing in the roots of the ash tree, the daggers of ice on the eaves – with larger, dimmer prospects. Tennyson recalls the days when he and Hallam used to walk and talk together:

> Till now the doubtful dusk reveal'd
> The knolls once more where, couch'd at ease,

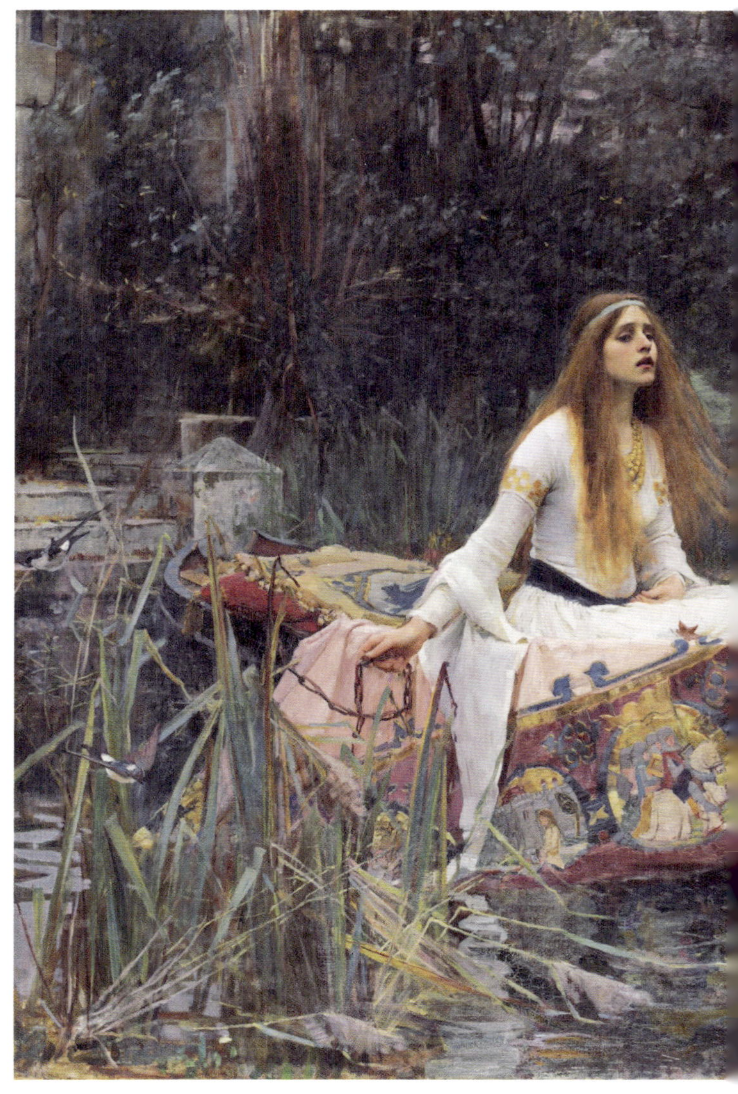

11. John William Waterhouse,
The Lady of Shalott, 1888. Oil on canvas.

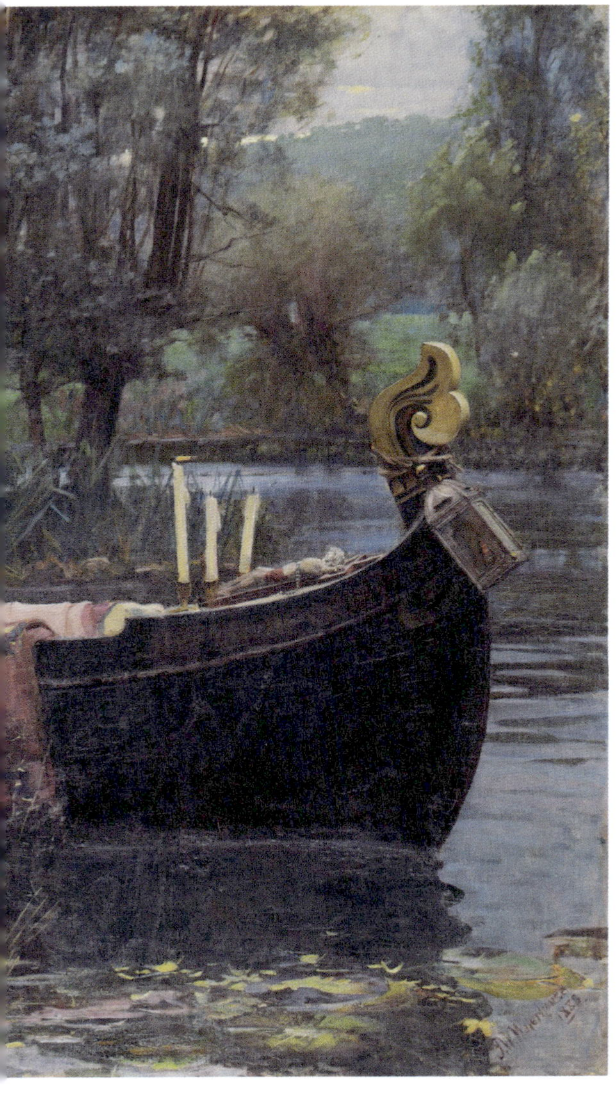

The white kine glimmer'd, and the trees
Laid their dark arms about the field:

And suck'd from out the distant gloom
A breeze began to tremble o'er
The large leaves of the sycamore,
And fluctuate all the still perfume,

And gathering freshlier overhead,
Rock'd the full-foliaged elms, and swung
The heavy-folded rose, and flung
The lilies to and fro, and said

'The dawn, the dawn,' and died away;
And East and West, without a breath,
Mixt their dim lights, like life and death,
To broaden into boundless day.

The landscape is made more dear by memories of Hallam:

I climb the hill: from end to end
Of all the landscape underneath,
I find no place that does not breathe
Some gracious memory of my friend;

No gray old grange, or lonely fold,
Or low morass and whispering reed,
Or simple stile from mead to mead,
Or sheep-walk up the windy wold;

No hoary knoll of ash and haw
That hears the latest linnet trill,
Nor quarry trench'd along the hill
And haunted by the wrangling daw;

No runlet tinkling from the rock;
Nor pastoral rivulet that swerves
To left and right thro' meadowy curves,
That feeds the mothers of the flock;

But each has pleased a kindred eye ...

The poet's mood colours the landscape so powerfully that it is hard to imagine anyone writing of these scenes in a more energetic tone: even his descriptions of the beauties of spring and renewal are softened by alliteration into a dreamy melancholy – the birds 'build and brood', the violets 'bud and blossom', the poet sees 'the light-blue lane of early dawn'. Tennyson can write in lively metre: 'The Brook' babbles along cheerfully enough in between its banks of blank verse, and 'The Charge of the Light Brigade' and 'The Revenge' could hardly be accused of languor. But the prevailing atmosphere is infectious: Lincolnshire pervades even Lyonesse and Camelot. Wherever historic Camelot may have been located, it is easy to see whence he drew these lines:

In the stormy east-wind straining,
The pale yellow woods were waning,
The broad stream in his banks complaining,

Heavily the low sky raining
Over tower'd Camelot;
Down she came and found a boat
Beneath a willow left afloat
And round about the prow she wrote
'The Lady of Shalott'.

Similarly, in the *Morte d'Arthur* the noise of battle may roll among the mountains by the wintry sea, but the landscape in its details is pure flat Lincolnshire: the many-knotted water flags 'that whistle stiff and dry about the marge' of the level lake, the incantatory music of the last lines –

Long stood Sir Bedivere
Revolving many memories, till the hull
Look'd one black dot against the verge of dawn,
And on the mere the wailing died away.

These are the sights and sounds of Lincolnshire, not of Lyonesse. The long, liquid, even Tennysonian line of iambic pentameter is the long, liquid, even line of the contours of the landscape: the master of onomatopoeia responds like an electrocardiograph to the heart's terrain.

Other writers describing Lincolnshire are full of Tennysonian echoes, inevitably. Dickens, the least enervating of writers, seems subdued by the scenery, and produces in *Bleak House* a dreariness that rivals the master's. Here is the opening description of Sir Leicester Dedlock's country house, Chesney Wold, in Chapter 2:

> The waters are out in Lincolnshire. The arch of the bridge in the park has been sapped and sopped away. The adjacent low-lying ground, for half a mile in breadth, is a stagnant river, with melancholy trees for islands in it, and a surface punctured all over, all day long, with falling rain ... The weather, for many a day and night, has been so wet that the trees seem wet through, and the soft loppings and prunings of the woodman's axe can make no crash or crackle as they fall. The deer, looking soaked, leave quagmires as they pass ... On Sundays, the little church in the park is mouldy; the oaken pulpit breaks out into a cold sweat; and there is a general smell and taste as of the ancient Dedlocks in their graves.

An acquired taste, perhaps, this kind of atmosphere – but Tennyson acquired it early, and passed it on to others. On leaving Somersby for Epping in 1837 he wrote to a friend, 'A known landskip is to me an old friend that continually talks to me of my own youth and half-forgotten things, and indeed does more for me than many an old friend that I know.' He is well aware of the complex intermingling of the real, the ideal and the imagined, and would probably not have been surprised to learn that without his guidance, many readers would find it hard to see the countryside as he saw it: his landscapes, despite their precision of detail, are highly personal, much more so than those of Wordsworth, whose grasp of the outer world was stronger, whose Lake District is there for all to see. The imagination is a powerful force, welding together the most unlikely components: for Tennyson (and, subsequently, for a generation of Victorian poets) even the bright, heroic, southern world of Homer could become imbued with the damp colours of the North Sea: in 'Mablethorpe' he writes on revisiting the town as a man,

> How often, when a child I lay reclined,
> I took delight in this locality!
> Here stood the infant Ilion of the mind,
> And here the Grecian ships did seem to be.
> And here again I come and only find
> The drain-cut levels of the marshy Lea –
> Gray sand banks and pale sunsets – dreary wind,
> Dim shores, dense rains, and heavy-clouded sea!

Matthew Arnold also saw English landscape through a classical filter, filling his poems with allusions to Arcady, commemorating his friend Clough under the name of Thyrsis. Unlike Tennyson, he was not country born: he was reared at Rugby, Winchester and Oxford. He celebrated both Rugby and Oxford in characteristically elegiac cadences, Rugby in the gloom of an autumn evening; Oxford, 'that sweet city with her dreaming spires', in these famous lines from *Essays in Criticism* (1865):

> Beautiful city! So venerable, so lovely, so unravaged by the fierce intellectual life of our century, so serene!... steeped in sentiment as she lies, spreading her gardens to the moonlight, and whispering from her towers the last enchantments of the Middle Age ...

> Adorable dreamer, whose heart has been so romantic!
> who has given thyself so prodigally, given thyself
> to sides and heroes not mine, only never to
> Philistines! home of lost causes, and forsaken beliefs,
> and unpopular names, and impossible loyalties!

Yet he also had a deep love of the countryside round Oxford, and in *The Scholar Gipsy* and 'Thyrsis the Sicilian' shepherds vie with English girls dancing round the Fyfield elm, and 'boys who in lone wheatfields scare the rooks'. Ilsley Down, Cumnor Hill, Bagley woods and Childsworth Farm hold their own with Thessaly and Enna, and the flora of the youthful Thames has never been so beautifully sung. Cowslips, bluebells, 'woods with anemones in flower till May', primroses, the spikes of purple orchises, the white flowering nettles, the pale pink convolvulus – it is almost too good to be true, too lush, too lovely, a landscape on the point of vanishing, a memory of a golden age. And so Arnold saw it: his poems are full of a sense of impending loss, a vague lament for passing glory, as well as a more precise lament for lost friends, lost youth.

Yet Arnold's sense of loss is very different from Wordsworth's. When Wordsworth wrote in the 'Ode on Intimations of Immortality',

> But there's a tree, of many, one
> A single field which I have looked upon,
> Both of them speak of something that is gone,

he is speaking of his own loss, not the world's: for him, nature endured, but man failed. Arnold's fears are larger, his faith less. We note in his verse the tone of hard-worked, weary modern man, seeking refreshment on weekend rambles, trying to find respite from 'this iron time / Of doubts, disputes, distractions, fears' ('Memorial Verses, to Wordsworth'). Arnold had the prosaic job of Inspector of Schools, and the prosaic public spirit and conscience of a Victorian public man. For him the country was not a way of life, as it was for Wordsworth, or a home, as it was for Tennyson – it was an evasion of the real business of existence, a consolation for the weekly grind, for the harsh statistics, the Blue Books on education, the ever-increasing speed and uncertainty he felt around him. Poetry was a refuge from this unpleasant world, and so was nature: she was 'the cool flowery lap of earth' where we had lain at birth, the womb to which man longed to return.

He longed, of course, in vain. Both Tennyson and Arnold turned to nature, the great comforter, on the death of loved friends; both sought a religious consolation in loved and familiar landscapes, endeared by the loved one. Yet nature did not truly console. The power of conviction that had sustained Wordsworth was slowly ebbing. Nature was not a god, nor was she even kindly: she did betray the hearts that loved her. Darwin revealed that she was red in tooth and claw. Tennyson cried,

> Are God and Nature then at strife,
> That Nature lends such evil dreams?

The God of Christianity and the Wordsworthian Great Being faded under the relentless questioning of science. Both Tennyson and Arnold were men of the new enlightenment, keenly interested in scientific discovery and progressive thought: they could not reject the new and alarming revelations of the nineteenth century, and Arnold at least could not fly 'the strange disease of modern life'. He was committed to waging war on modern ugliness and Philistinism, on the brick terraces of Margate – and, thus committed, he had no choice but to keep them in view. The conclusion of 'Thyrsis' sums it up: he has been forced to abandon the hopes youth, the landscapes glimmer only in ghostly italics from beyond the grave:

Too rare, too rare, grow now my visits here!
'Mid city-noise, not, as with thee of yore,
Thyrsis! in reach of sheep-bells is my home.
– Then through the great town's harsh,
heart-wearying roar,
Let in thy voice a whisper often come,
To chase fatigue and fear:
Why faintest thou? I wander'd till I died.
Roam on! The light we sought is shining still.
Dost thou ask proof? Our tree yet crowns the hill,
Our Scholar travels yet the loved hill-side.

BIBLIOGRAPHY

S. Baring-Gould, *The Vicar of Morwenstow*, London, 1876
John Barrell, *The Dark Side of the Landscape: The Rural Poor in English Painting 1730–1840*, Cambridge, 1980
-- and John Bull, *The Idea of Landscape and the Sense of Place, 1730–1840*, Cambridge, 1972
Kenneth Clark, *Landscape into Art*, London, 1949
Dorothy Eagle and Hilary Carnell, *The Oxford Literary Guide to the British Isles*, Oxford, 1977
Margaret Gelling, *Signposts to the Past: Place Names and the History of England*, London, 1978
Valerie Grosvenor Myer, *Jane Austen in her Age*, London, 1979
W. G. Hoskins, *The Making of the English Landscape*, London, 1955
Christopher Hussey, *The Picturesque*, London, 1927, 1967
K. H. Jackson, ed., *A Celtic Miscellany: Translations from the Celtic Literatures*, London, 1951
Desmond King-Hele, *Doctor of Revolution: The Life and Genius of Erasmus Darwin*, London, 1977
Lucien Leclaire, *General Analytical Bibliography of the Regional Novelists of the British Isles 1800–1950*, Paris, 1954
J. G. Lockhart, *Life of Burns*, London, 1828
Edward Malins, *English Landscaping and Literature 1660–1840*, Oxford, 1966
E. W. Manwaring, *Italian Landscape in Eighteenth Century England*, London, 1925
Norman Nicholson, *The Lake District: An Anthology*, London, 1977
Carola Oman, *The Wizard of the North*, London, 1973
Charles Peake, *Poetry of the Landscape and the Night*, London, 1967
Thomas Pennant, *Tours in Wales*, London, 1810
Canon H. D. Rawnsley, *Literary Associations of the English Lakes*, Glasgow, 1894
C. B. L. Tennyson, *Alfred Tennyson*, London, 1949
Raymond Williams, *The Country and the City*, London, 1973

LIST OF ILLUSTRATIONS

Measurements are given height before width, cm followed by inches

1, 6. James Ward, *The Eildon Hills and The Tweed*, 1807. Oil on panel, 103 × 173 × 2.80 (40⅝ × 68⅛ × 1⅛). Bequest of Sir Theophilus Biddulph 1948; received 1969. Scottish National Gallery, Edinburgh (NG 2306) **2.** Claude Lorrain glasses: coloured viewing glasses used by landscape painters, 1800–24. Photo SSPL/Getty Images **3.** Benjamin Robert Haydon, *William Wordsworth* (or *Wordsworth on Helvellyn*), 1842. Oil on canvas, 124.5 × 99.1 (49⅛ × 39⅛). National Portrait Gallery, London (NPG 1857) **4.** Dorothy Wordsworth, journal entry of 15 April 1802, *Grasmere journal*. Pen and ink on paper, 14.8 × 9.5 (5⅞ × 3¾). Wordsworth Trust, Grasmere. Photo Bridgeman Images **5.** Samuel Taylor Coleridge, sketch map of the Lake District, in his notebook of 1802. British Library archive, London (Add. 47497) **7.** Fay Godwin, Top Withens, near Haworth, Yorkshire, 1977. British Library, London (FG3017-1). Photo via Bridgeman Images. © The British Library Board **8.** Charlotte Brontë, 'There once was a little girl, and her name was Ane', miniature manuscript with watercolour drawings of a seascape and a woman out walking, 1828. Bronte Parsonage Museum, Haworth. Photo Bronte Parsonage Museum/Bridgeman Images **9.** Richard Wilson, *Snowdon* [Yr Wyddfa] *from Llyn Nantlle*, 1765–66. Oil on canvas, 101 × 127 (39¾ × 50). Walker Art Gallery, Liverpool (WAG 2429) **10.** J. M. W. Turner, *Tintagel Castle from the Sea*, *c.* 1825. Gouache and watercolour on paper, 18.1 × 23 (7¼ × 9⅛). Tate, London (D25470) **11.** John William Waterhouse, *The Lady of Shalott*, 1888. Oil on canvas, 153 × 200 (60¼ × 78¾). Tate, London (N01543).

ALSO AVAILABLE IN THE POCKET PERSPECTIVES SERIES:

Julian Bell on Painting

John Boardman on The Parthenon

T. J. Clark on Bruegel

E. H. Gombrich on Fresco Painting

James Hall on The Self-Portrait

Lucy R. Lippard on Pop Art

Linda Nochlin on The Body

Griselda Pollock on Gauguin

Richard Rogers on Modern Architecture

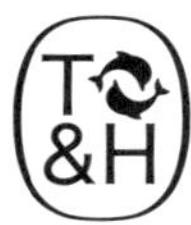

Be the first to know about our new releases,
exclusive content and author events by visiting
thamesandhudson.com
thamesandhudsonusa.com
thamesandhudson.com.au

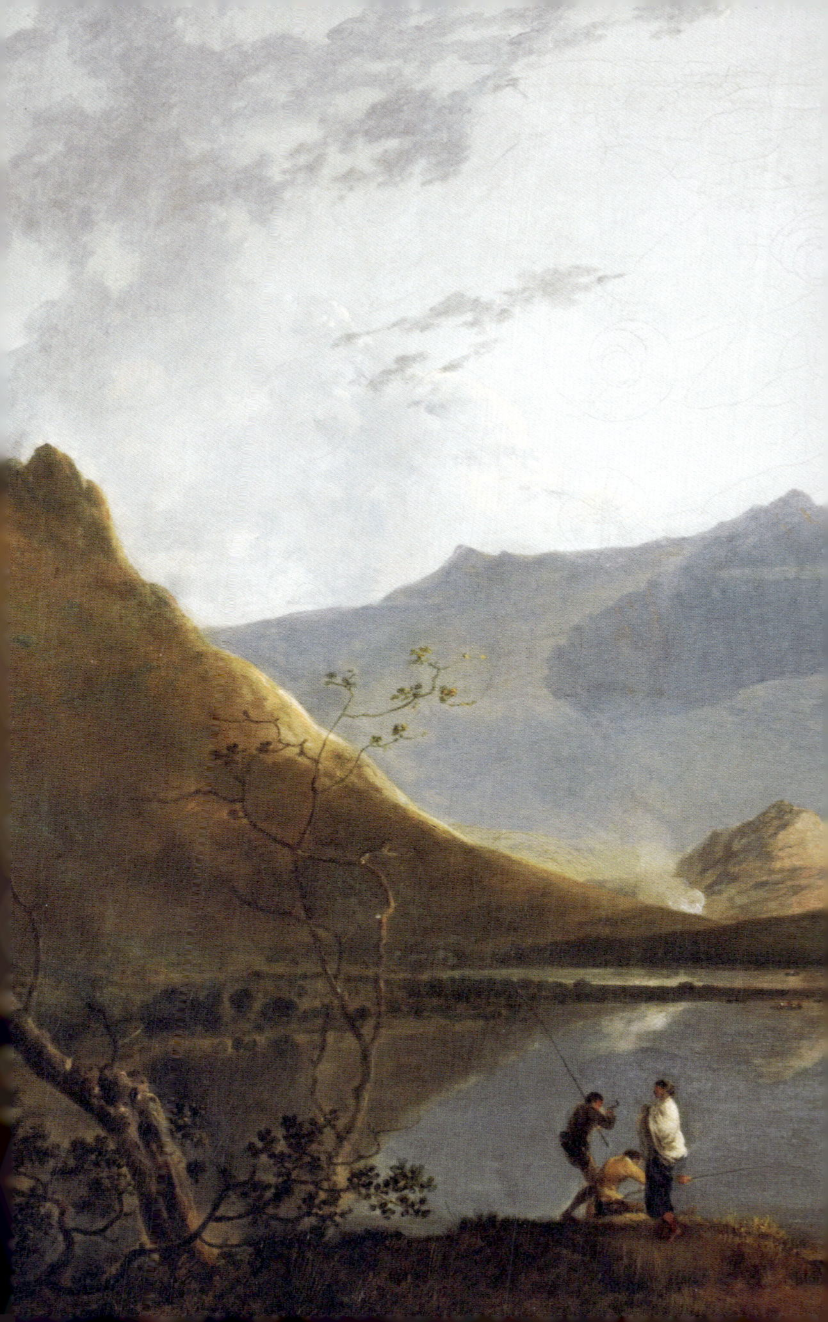